Go Girl Go!

REAL STORIES OF NEW ZEALAND WOMEN IN BUSINESS

By Jacqui Thomas

JT Publishing Company Ltd

© JT Publishing Company Ltd
First Published 2001

ISBN 0-473-07514-8

Layout by Niche Tourism Design Ltd, Queenstown, New Zealand
Printed by John McIndoe Ltd, Dunedin, New Zealand

Publisher: JT Publishing Company Ltd
P O Box 115, Queenstown, New Zealand
jacforwords@xtra.co.nz
jeffturner@xtra.co.nz

Photography
by Cay Cassini

Cover Art
by Minhal al Halabi

Foreword
by Helen Clark,
Prime Minister of New Zealand

Acknowledgements

A huge thank you to the many people who have
supported this project – To Noel Coutts for inspiring the concept
and pushing me along when ever I needed it;
To Jeff Turner for believing in the project and helping me
see it through to the end;
To Minhal al Halabi for stepping in with his
creative genius to paint the cover;
To Ally Mondillo and Lindsay Collins at Niche Design
for their overall design expertise and for happily
answering all my blonde questions;
To Helen Clark and the people of her office
for so promptly supplying a thoughtful and inspiring foreword;
To Cay Cassini for travelling the length of the country to
capture the women of the book photographically;
To Dave Sissing at Kodak for supplying film to an unknown project;
To Chris Wilson at Hannafins for his enthusiastic support
in developing and printing the photos;
To Dave Laurent at Happy Snappa, Queenstown for his support;
To Jay Cassells for his advice and answers to more blonde questions;
To Jenny McLeod for her experience and advice;
To all my family and friends for their constant encouragement over the
past eighteen months and for pestering me to get the book finished;
And of course, to all the women who shared their personal stories
to make the project possible.

Thank you!

*For Tracey – a bold, brave, beautiful woman
who I love, respect and admire.
A real gutsy lady who would be in this book
if she wasn't so far away!*

 **Prime Minister**

Foreword

The days of a woman's place being in the home are long gone, in New Zealand at least.

Annette King, Sandra Lee, Margaret Wilson, Lianne Dalziel, Marian Hobbs and Laila Harré serve with me in the Cabinet, and Phillida Bunkle, Judith Tizard and Tariana Turia in the wider ministry. Marie Shroff, as the Cabinet Secretary, is one of New Zealand's most senior public servants, as is Karen Poutasi, the Director-General of Health. Silvia Cartwright, soon to be our second women governor-general, and Sian Elias, the present Chief Justice, have achieved much in the law, as have women like Theresa Gattung and Wendy Pye in the world of business. In the arts, Kiri Te Kanawa, Malvina Major and Keri Hulme are internationally celebrated.

We are part of the post-war generation which came of age when women's abilities received more recognition and have enjoyed opportunities that were not open to our mothers and grandmothers. We have been able to blaze a path for younger women to come along in much greater numbers.

Despite the example of women like Theresa and Wendy, the business sector has proven perhaps the most difficult area for women to rise in. But the glass ceiling is coming down. What this book does is highlight the achievements of a growing number of women in the tough world of business. It provides insights into the efforts required for them to achieve: the sheer hard work, the obstacles that must be overcome and the fulfilment that comes from attaining one's goals.

I hope books like this provide the inspiration for ever greater numbers of women to succeed in the world of business and commerce. I am confident it will.

Helen Clark
Prime Minister

CONTENTS

INTRODUCTION

This project started back in 1999 through my own frustrations as a newly self-employed writer. After completing a journalism course by correspondence I'd decided I didn't want to go and work for a newspaper or a magazine – I wanted to freelance. This seemed easy enough and I was sure it was the answer to my dreams of freedom. I started writing and soon I had a few regular contracts and I was surviving, but only just. The hardest part was not the writing but the business side of it - knowing what to charge for my work, getting agreements from people, sorting out taxes and accounting procedures. I bluffed my way through blindly for months not wanting to ask anybody for help for fear of confirming to them that I really didn't know what I was doing!

One day I came home to my partner frustrated and upset. I felt I had no idea what I was supposed to be doing and said to him "It's so hard. You can't just go into Whitcoulls and buy a book on it". "That's your answer," he said. "Write a book for women about getting started in business." That upset me even more, how was I supposed to write a book for the rest of the world when I didn't know what I was doing myself? "That's easy," he said. "Go and talk to successful business women and ask them how they got started." My initial reaction was 'what a cheek!' – how rude to ask these successful women to share their secrets! But the more I thought about it, the more it seemed like a good idea.

When I first sent twenty letters out to successful business women I knew of in my area, I expected about five to be interested in my project. I hoped for ten. Eighteen of those women were happy to be interviewed – the response was overwhelming! The first thing I learnt through this project is that most people are happy to help you – you just have to be brave enough to ask! I took my search nationwide and was met with the same enthusiasm. After interviewing about sixty amazing women, all with fantastic stories to tell, I realised I had to stop, it was getting harder and harder to choose which stories to include in this book.

I've endeavoured to select fifteen stories as vastly different from one another as possible, incorporating different types of businesses, age groups, ethnic groups, geographical locations and personal circumstances. A big thank you to all the women who took the time to share their experiences with me. I learned from each and every one of you. Now I hope others will be inspired and motivated and learn from the stories shared in this book.

Enjoy!

Lynette "Polly" McFadden

Lynette "Polly" McFadden

HARCOURTS REAL ESTATE

Lynette, known as Polly to her friends, is a vibrant Maori woman successfully operating several Harcourts real estate offices in the Christchurch area. A working class background hasn't stopped her from becoming one of Christchurch's hottest businesswomen. Not content with her own success, she shares her positive energy with all around her, inspiring others to succeed and grow into whatever they wish to become.

I come from a family background that is absolutely not business aware. My family doesn't have a single business brain among them. My parents are very traditional Maori, working class folks. They are very loving, but very traditional role models. Mum was at home looking after the kids, while Dad went out to work. They had us when they were about twenty, so they were quite young and carefree, and probably didn't really settle until they were much older. By that time I was about twenty and had needed some guidance a bit earlier than that. I had a real issue with achieving but looking back I think I was just trying to get my parents to notice me. They were just drifting along in life and I wanted more, I never wanted to drift.

I was very driven at school. With the absence of role models I wasn't really sure where I was going, so I went nursing after I finished school. I did really well in my school exams and retrospectively I would have preferred law, but that just seemed far too outrageous to even be considered. It probably still would be quite unheard of for someone from our family to do law. So I went nursing, which was deemed very good and very special. I enjoyed my nursing and made some special friends but eventually I got tired of it. After twelve years of nursing, I was away with my husband and said to him ' I don't wish to go back nursing, I wish to do something else'. We'd been married ten years and had our first son, Harry. He thought I'd be good at real estate. We'd always bought and sold properties, done them up as investments. It seemed like a natural progression.

It was 1994 when I decided to start selling real estate. Harry was only little, he wasn't even walking or talking, and I was deciding to work fulltime. The role models around me in real estate were very poor at the time. I was quite shocked because I'd come from a very disciplined background. Nursing is very formal and structured and hierarchical. In nursing, if something is supposed to be done at a certain time, it is. In real estate there were no firm rules or boundaries, which I didn't relate to very well. I was quite formal and extraordinarily diligent, which my colleagues struggled with a bit, but the sales started to come. I still place a huge emphasis on service, going the extra mile for clients.

In my first year in real estate, I was among the top Canterbury salespeople and had a six figure income. I also had a change of office in my first year, which didn't really work out. I looked across the road and thought I saw something better, but it wasn't, so I had to go back to my old boss with my tail between my legs, and he kindly took me back. I had a couple of years of good sales and then John, my husband, decided he was sick of plumbing and he wanted to join me in real estate. He came and worked with me for a while which was really hard because I was used to doing my own thing, and had been for a couple of years. I had systems and routines established and he was coming in and mucking it all up. He'd constantly be asking me what I was doing and where I was going. It was pretty tough initially, until he got on his feet, which he did quite quickly, thankfully!

After three years selling, I reached a point where I was dissatisfied. I felt there was something lacking in the business we were working in. I guess I got to a point where I felt I could do it better, and I felt my boss was taking me for granted. I left and so did my husband and two colleagues, Judy Curnow and Bruce Newman. We left our businesses, the people we were working for, which was huge for them because big agents walking out the door is tough on a business.

We bought a business that was vacant, the Papanui Harcourts office. It was vacant because the previous owner had killed himself, and the owner before that had run it down. We inherited a business that was very 'rough around the edges' but we believed we could make a go of it. It was difficult and extraordinarily expensive. It took every last resource we had. We bought the office and walked into a meeting with about ten sales people. Three of those got up and left. We'd paid hundreds of thousands of dollars for this office with a history where someone had just killed himself, three of the staff just walked out the door, and a total of seventeen listings. What had we done? I remember going into my office and crying, thinking we'd made a dreadful mistake.

But, we made it work. We had a really good year, we built up the team, we acquired another office and we sold property. The four partners didn't just concentrate on administration. We administrated, plus we sold hard to try and get the capital up in the business. We attracted other people that liked our energy. We changed the name to Harcourts Gold, because it symbolised a special quality and gave us a stamp of permanence. It went with our philosophy of being outstanding.

The vision behind the business is driven by me. I'm the dreamer, the philosopher, the person who directs where the business is going. I am terrible at the bookwork, the finance side of it. I hate that aspect. I love the momentum and the drive and the opportunity to take people out of their comfort zones and along a new path. We started with the Papanui office and then acquired the Redwood office. This was another office that was rapidly going downhill, so again it was hard work. We had a big reputation at that stage, but other agents still looked sideways at us, we weren't quite trusted. We had broken the mould. We had gone from being agents to people who owned businesses.

We weren't helped at all, not by anybody. I think that's the nature of the business. Real estate is a competitive business, which fears sharing, which I think is disappointing. I think women in business are more accustomed to sharing their ideas, visions and goals, and they tend to realise that everyone picks up the same task and goes about it differently. In real estate there is a fear of someone else getting in first, so you don't tell anyone anything.

We've now incorporated two other offices. We may consider growing more in the future but at the moment it's a major job keeping this ship on course. I see my job as plotting the course. I am the mentor, the coach, the dreamer, the teacher. Other people tidy up the financial detail that I'm not interested in around me.

Working with my husband is interesting. Of course there are times when I think 'Geez, you're a pain in the arse', but most of the time I think how fantastic it is that I get to work with this man who I absolutely adore. In sales and motivation and working with all sorts of people you really have to do a lot of headwork. Real estate, or any sort of sales success, isn't just about product knowledge it's about what goes on in your head. I think a lot of the skills I've learned have transpired into other areas of our lives. I'm grateful for the opportunities the business has provided to add a real depth to our relationship. But, make no bones about it, there are times when I could just scream, because it is hard yakka. There is also a tug of war between us at times, which is not necessarily a good thing, but I'm being honest. There is a power struggle that exists when a husband and wife work beside each other. And there are times when I will step back and think 'oh, just let this one go.'

Our roles are quite clearly defined. John deals with the administration and manages the office. I do the mentoring, training, coaching. I provide the vision, the goals. Really, he does the left brain stuff and I do the right.

The transition from sales agent to management has been fun. There's a big workload, though and a lot more dynamics to think about. When you're selling it's just you and the people you're selling for. When you go into management, it's you and the people you sell for, you and the people that sell for you, you and the bank manager. There's a lot more happening, and you have to move quickly and be very sure of your decisions. It's been very challenging and very rewarding.

We have four Harcourts offices. Harcourts is a franchise and our offices have become some of the top New Zealand franchises for turnover. Sales volume is very high and there is a strong marketing push. I handle our marketing and it's very out there. We've caused a lot of ripples and probably a lot of headaches for other companies who have chosen to sit back. We are very aggressive about the way we take our message to the public because I don't want to be controlled by the market. I don't want to think about sales going down because lawyers might start selling, or because there's going to be a change in government. I know there are always people out there who want to buy and sell properties and I want to deal with them. I'm more keen to be out there searching for the business rather than sitting around thinking that the market is quiet, or its winter and nobody sells. I don't buy into those excuses.

One of the things I love about being your own boss is that supposedly you can take as much time off as you like. The flip side of that is you don't, in fact you rarely take any time off at all. You can take time off and go away, but you're never really away. That's probably one of the challenges that my husband and I both struggle with, even when we're overseas people still phone us, fax us, or whatever, and we are always wondering if everything is OK.

Another example with two opposite sides to the coin is when you go out, you get wondrous service because people know you, or they think you'll look after them, which is fantastic, but the flipside is you can't just go out with your family and have your own personal space. You can't yell at each other if you want to, or pop down to the shops looking gross. Not that I go to a lot of fuss, but I think it is important to look smart in the public eye. That doesn't mean I get all done up in a suit. My idea of smart has altered a lot. I'm not as formal as I used to be. I think that has come with increased confidence.

The main advantage of being your own boss is that it's wonderful to be responsible for your own income. I can't stress that enough. It is wonderful to think "I will earn what I am worth" rather than 'I will get what I am given'. I can't imagine going back into a situation now where I will get what somebody else decides to pay me. We can earn whatever we would wish for. I do try to keep that quite real though, because money has never been a huge motivator for me. For me the sense of recognition has been a more major motivator. I just think if you do it right the money will come anyway, which infuriates my husband. He's always saying 'it's not in the bloody stars, you have to get out and work hard'. And I do work hard, but it's not the money that drives me. I believe the money side of it will happen on its own.

Professional advice has been hugely important in our business. I think a lot of what I do is from my own wisdom but that's not enough. In business you need help, you need a good accountant and you need good legal advice. When we set up our first office it cost us $25,000 just to do the partnership agreement. It wasn't until one of the partners tried to leave and things got scrappy that we realised how good the partnership agreement was. You need help and I also feel you need to be challenged. You need someone to say 'have you thought about this, have you thought about that'. I definitely feel professional help is important. Being successful in business is hard work. You just can't row your own boat all the time. You have to get people helping. Sometimes you need someone to tow you, sometimes you need a push start, sometimes you just need someone swimming gently beside you while you row, but don't try and row your wee boat all alone, it's too tough.

I've had some major influences in my life but my main focus is still my family. My husband, John, our two boys, my Mum, my Dad and my sister are all hugely important to me. I had a brother as well who died from a heroin overdose. I do carry that loss with me, not sadly as a piece of baggage, but as a reminder that life is special.

Balancing family and business is hard work. But I don't feel in my heart that our boys have missed out on anything because of it. They have two loving parents that adore them. I spend as much time with them as I can and really value that time. When I first started in real estate Harry was only little. We've just had Louie and I worked right through that pregnancy which wasn't too bad. I was quite small so it wasn't much of an issue. I had to come back to work straight away which was quite hard, but a commercial reality. I do juggle a lot of different hats, and I think I do pretty well at keeping the balance. I don't feel guilty about it. I do the best I can with what I have. The main problem for me comes from other people, the judgements that other women make like 'isn't it a shame you're not home with your baby'. I think "cute" - I'm home in the morning and I hug him to bits, I'm there in the afternoon, we bath together, I listen to him, I whisper in his ears about his ancestors, and I call on my grandparents to protect him. It is tough to get a balance, but everyday I work on it. I don't feel guilty about not spending more time with my children. I just wish other people would understand we do what we do, and we do the best we can. And, my best is pretty darn good!

I have a wondrous nanny and that has helped me a lot. To be free to be successful in business you need to have the home front sorted. You can't do everything. There's no point running yourself ragged thinking 'I've got to be home breastfeeding, and the washing's piling up and what are we going to have for dinner'. Get some help and use your support systems.

Something that women in business have in their favour is their intuition. Listen to that inner voice, that gut instinct that guides you from within. If I said that to a man he'd think 'what the hell is she on about now'. But women have that intuitive sense, we need to trust that inner voice and listen to it. I am a very spiritual person.

My grandparents guide me through life and protect me. Listening to my inner voice is like having these people I trust and respect close to me. I completely trust my intuition and I'm incredibly forthright about it. If something feels wrong, it is wrong. If I like something, I'm over the top gushy about it, but it's not a pretence, that's what I feel. I like to keep my emotions close to the surface. I don't like them to be buried. I think if you bury your emotions too deep you forget where they are and I won't live my life like that.

Being positive is also important. You can't take rejection too personally. When you get knocked back you just have to pick yourself up, dust yourself off and carry on. You can't take rejection on board. People feed off positive energy. They don't want to know about the loan you have to pay off, or any of your personal dramas, they want you to instil faith in them with your optimism.

Positive energy is something I look for when we're recruiting staff. I'm often the last person involved in our recruitment process. The other partners ask a lot of questions and check the person out, then if they get past two of my partners I'll take a look. There are people who stand out and I think I'm better able to pick those people. People are attracted to similar energy. Negative people tend to stick together within their own comfort zone. Other people are inspired and motivated by different energy. I think that one of the God given gifts I have is an energy that can carry people where they wish to go. It's like an embrace should we meet, it will keep you warm and safe and inspire you to succeed. That's what I aim for when choosing our staff.

One thing I really impress on all our staff is the importance of service. I place a huge emphasis on going the extra mile for our customers. If you think about money before people they will sense it. I've always thought about the people first and believed that the money will follow and it has. I have never taken people's business for granted and I hope I never do. I try as much as possible to call our customers just to say thank you, 'thank you for giving us your business'. I have never stopped thanking people for choosing us. I go into businesses sometimes that have long since lost touch with what it feels like to be a customer and I refuse to do that. When I'm out and about I notice everything, I assess and analyse. I think about what makes this restaurant successful and the one across the road empty. I look at what stands out and think about how we could use those aspects in our business.

There don't seem to be a lot of Maori women in business. But, having said that I've just recently been up to the Maori Women's Business Awards and met some very atypical Maori women, really stunning businesswomen, so they are around. There are a lot of Maori women coming through the universities and choosing professions, but not that many in business. But, there are more and more, so I'm enjoying meeting them and getting to know them.

I don't feel there are huge issues being a Maori woman in the business world. For me the issues are more on a personal level. Things like I want to go the extra mile for Maori families. I tend to want to help them with their problems. A recent example is a Maori woman with a gambling problem wanting me to sell her home. I was concerned she would lose the funds and then what would happen to her children? So I do have quiet, personal issues as a Maori woman in business.

I do think it's really good to be a positive role model out in the community. I went to speak at Aranui High School a while ago and really tried to get across to the kids that what you see isn't how I started. You don't have to be born with a silver spoon in your mouth, you don't have to have parents that are doctors or lawyers. You can start with anything. My father was an incredibly staunch, working man, you didn't mess with him. I know that touched those kids because they come from similar backgrounds. I don't have any problem at all telling people that's the background I come from, I think it's a good thing. It's given me the ability to deal with people from all walks of life, from all positions, and I do. Right from when I started a lot of my sales came from very upper bracket people. I didn't take any crap but I also conceded a great deal to them in terms of service and it didn't worry me. I think that was refreshing for them.

Success is out there, it's out there for all of us. You just have to want it and it will come. I see it quite simply. It is hard work but the actual ingredients for success are very simple.

Jane
Lucas

Jane Lucas

BJ'S HEALTH & FITNESS CENTRES LTD

Jane started her career as a farmer's wife teaching a few local ladies aerobics in the country. Thirteen years later she's recognised as a successful businesswoman, owning and operating three health & fitness centres in the Nelson / Marlborough region.

Back in 1987 when I first started, it was quite hard for women to achieve their goals in business. I came from a small farming community and was happily married to a farmer. I was quite content. Life was good. I didn't have any burning desire to do anything different. I certainly didn't wake up one morning thinking 'my goodness, there must be more to life than this'. I had three young children, one of which was still at home. I kept busy, we did a lot of entertaining and I belonged to many small community groups and always ended up on various committees. It's interesting, once you're a mother your organisational skills are honed towards working things out and fitting everything in. Life was always so busy. I think women have an advantage in that respect, we tend to have very good organisational skills, even more so once you have children.

I did a lot of social things. I also used to play badminton. One day at the club someone approached me from Nelson and asked me if I'd be interested in teaching aerobics. At home I discussed it with my husband to see how he felt about it. He laughed and said I was far too old. Of course that was like red rag to a bull! Away I went to do the training and I started teaching aerobics.

It was great. I was feeling really good because I was getting fitter and shedding kilos. I started teaching in Nelson and then got the job of running the aerobics at the YMCA in Richmond. I was the only instructor and had a very small group of ladies who really enjoyed my classes. It was very social and we'd often have a coffee afterwards. We had quite a few problems there, though, with the manager forgetting to open the centre for us, or the mats would be locked away in a different place. I seemed to be constantly apologising. My customers were very loyal but it was embarrassing. And, to make it worse, just across the road was the local, very well patronised 'Jazzercise' class. I'd walk back to the carpark after the class with my half a dozen ladies, and look into this room chock-a-block full of leotard clad women. (Little was I to know then that within three years I would take over the Les Mills Jazzercise franchise when the hall based classes found it difficult to compete with a gym offering everything.)

My ladies were very loyal and one day one of them said to me, 'why don't you find a place of your own, so we don't keep having these problems here?' In my stupid naïve way I thought 'yeah, that's a great idea'.

I found an upstairs area that had a beautiful sprung timber floor, perfect for aerobics. The building was 100 years old. I contacted the landlord but there was a problem, he already had someone interested. The other guy wanted to open a gym, so he thought we might be able to share the area and the lease. So we did. Brian arrived with his gym equipment and I arrived with my aerobic ladies. I was in business!

Brian wasn't into advertising and marketing but I really needed to get the word out. As it was Brian's gym and Jane's aerobics studio, I came up with BJ's. The arrangement with Brian worked for a while until my classes started getting bigger and I needed all 50% of my space for a couple of hours a day. There was tension and I started getting concerned that this partnership of lease was not going to work. I made a mental note never to go into partnership again. It all came to a head when Brian had a disagreement with the landlord and was asked to leave. I was left with the whole area, which was great, but also the whole lease to pay and a husband who was wondering why I wasn't home, which wasn't so great. I'd told him it was just going to be a part time thing, but all of a sudden I had financial commitments and I was going to have to work a lot harder to meet them. I had to really think about how I was going to make it pay.

So I started a modelling business. I utilized all the talent I could find in the area, beauticians, hairdressers, fashion experts, and I set up a modelling studio in part of the space. I ran evening courses covering deportment, beauty and catwalk training and organised fashion shows at the weekends, as well as taking up to 15 aerobics classes a week. My children thought the place was their second home! It was a real family business with my mother-in-law sewing leotards and tights and selling them at the gym and my children helping out with reception duties. Things started looking better with increasing numbers attending classes giving me the ability to employ more instructors. It was about then I took over the Les Mills franchise so I had trained instructors coming out my ears. Up until then we had to send instructors to Christchurch to attend training which was costly and time consuming.

The next thing I wanted to offer was a circuit class, which were becoming increasingly popular in other gyms. This meant I needed money to buy equipment. My husband helped by making some gear on the farm but I still needed money to purchase the rest of the equipment I needed and also more space in the building.

I had to go cap in hand to the bank manager and ask for a loan. They had no problem lending the money but it was with the family farm as security. No way did I want to ask the family to do that as what I was doing was slightly frowned upon anyway. So, I applied to run government funded Access courses. The courses were aimed at school leavers to prepare themselves for job interviews and future work. I had seen what the modelling courses had achieved in boosting confidence and self-esteem so I based the course on those. The difference was that these courses ran all day for six weeks with twelve participants!

The first day I walked in to find twelve young ladies waiting and looking bored, was the first of many times I was totally overcome with self-doubt. "What was I doing? I'm a total fraud and I'm sure they can tell. Why don't I go back to being a 100% committed farmer's wife… there was nothing wrong with it!" But the first course came and went and many more followed. My confidence grew and so did the need for space.

I took on an extra room, so I had the whole top floor. I had circuits running in one room, aerobics at the other end of it, and the gym in another room. I also had a beautician, a massage therapist and sunbeds as well as the modelling / Access area. It sounds grand but it wasn't. Being old and timber the whole building used to shake during an aerobics class. Many a time my beautician's client would appear from her room looking pale and convinced she'd just experienced a large earthquake! But it was fun and many hours were spent painting and doing it up. It was what I could afford, and at that stage there really wasn't much money to be made in the gym industry. I eventually did find a bank manager who was prepared to give me an unsecured loan based on projected income – I could have kissed his feet!

I think one of the things that hold women back in business, generally, is a fear of loans. A lot of men race in and buy or lease the best, never considering failure, and often they don't need to worry because it works out. Women are nest builders. Women in my generation didn't usually go into business themselves until after they'd had a family, and even then it wasn't really socially acceptable. They were used to budgeting the shopping every week and I think a lot of women still shiver when they think about bank loans. They worry more than men about how they're going to pay them off and the consequences of not being able to. As you become more confident with your product in business, your general confidence grows and it becomes easier to spend money. You do have to spend money to make money. I am still spending. The fitness industry has gone from strength to strength over the last twelve years. The customer expects more – better equipment, nicer facilities, car parking space, pristine bathrooms, but you are able to charge a fee that reflects what you offer. The days of a couple of dumb-bells and a squat machine on bare boards and a loo in the corner have gone.

Every time I open a new business I am besieged with doubt and I always ask myself 'why am I doing this?' Many times I've wondered what my life would've been like if I was still on the farm baking cakes. Generally I'm happy whatever I'm doing. I'm not striving to be number one, top cat, businesswoman of the year, or anything like that. I wanted to give good service but most of the time it was sheer survival mode. For me it helped being a woman at the start as so many people, male and female, had no faith in women in business. This inspired a stubborn critter like me with a, not necessarily sensible, "I'll show them" attitude.

When I think 'business', it conjures up images of making lots of money and being successful. I certainly wasn't doing that in the early years so I didn't really think of it as a business. It was, obviously, because I had all these bills to pay. I did get support from home, but I always felt a bit guilty about being a lousy wife and mother. It was a selfish thing to do. I changed over the years and nothing can really stop that happening. Our relationship wasn't strong enough to cope with those changes, and by mutual agreement our marriage ended.

The positive has always been that my children haven't suffered from being raised by a slightly pre-occupied, always busy, never at home, mother. I'm sure the family farm and their father's dependability during the early years helped. They are three independent, happy children who are all doing well at university. Thank heaven for that!

I finally moved out of the old timber BJ's building. The new building was an old car sales yard. It required funds to renovate and the old gym equipment was looking shabby. I borrowed money to purchase new equipment and at the same time took over another struggling Richmond gym, which provided me with more equipment. All the extra space meant the luxury of separate rooms for circuits and aerobics, plus made to measure rooms for the beautician and sunbeds. It was and still is a great building and it doesn't shake during class! It was great to be able to give the loyal people who'd supported me through the early years something that was a bit nicer, classier.

I can remember the night before we opened that gym. We had an amazing rain storm and discovered all these leaks in the roof! We had done a big advertising feature for the newspaper, the Mayor was invited to cut the ribbon and the local radio station were "going live" and the rain continued to pour down. Water was literally running down the walls of the gym! But, when people start buying memberships you can forget about anything.

The only business plan I ever did was when we entered a Commerce Nelson competition for best new business. We didn't win but it gave me a good opportunity to sit down with my good friend and accountant, Anne. She was in the first class I ever took at BJ's with her boss Bronwyn…just the two of them…no-one else! Over the years I've seen more of Anne up a ladder with a paintbrush helping to renovate than I have sitting behind her desk. She has been a great support through the many ups and downs of my business and personal life. So, Anne and I sat down and thought about where BJ's should be in five years time. I always wanted a gym in Nelson, but I never imagined there would eventually be one in Blenheim, too.

I think a good point about being a woman in business is that you need the support of your colleagues and staff. You will always get that in a small group. It's only when you expand that people's attitudes may change, they start to feel threatened. When I first started I was taking all the classes, but then I was able to afford up to ten instructors. When I started taking the new circuit classes, they didn't want to lose any of their aerobics customers, which was understandable for them but not for the business, so there were a few fallouts. As you get bigger and don't get the same support, it can get quite threatening. You're suddenly a boss rather than a friend. I think women take that on board more than men do. You have to become more aloof and not share everything with your staff. The big family atmosphere disappears.

I think you still need to work with them, hands on, though for happier staff relations. That does make things difficult if you want to pull away slightly from the business. The dynamics seem to work better if you are physically there. As I started to pull away a little bit, I did notice cracks appearing. The staff want you there, and the customers like to see you there as well. Customers started saying 'Jane's never here these days' as though I didn't care about them, which is not true. I really do care about them, but it gets harder to show that with three gyms all open from 6am until 8.30pm every day.

I think with gyms, because it's a people business, you do put in a lot of effort for the members. I don't mean to sound like I've made huge self sacrifices, but you work hard to build up good customer relations. I get a lot of positive feedback, which is great, as I want people to enjoy everything we offer. I think I've always got more out of this business in terms of satisfaction than money. The downside is that criticism hurts, and I take it personally - I still hate opening the suggestion box!

I have three gyms now, in Richmond , Nelson and Blenheim and my life has changed once again. I have very happily remarried. My new husband travels a lot with his business and as I want to be with him I have had to restructure my business. We have bought a house in Australia where we like to spend five months of the year, which I adore. I tried putting temporary managers into the gyms, but that wasn't very successful. Unless they have a real interest in the business they are never going to sweat blood like you do, which is understandable. I had a man approach me some years ago asking to be involved with BJ's. He was the owner of the other Nelson gym. I've known him for years, he used to be a member of BJ's in Richmond. At the time I didn't want to hand over the reins. Your business becomes an identity. If I'm out socially, people will always talk to me about the gym. My business gives me confidence in social situations.

So I was a bit scared about getting rid of part of myself by giving away some of my business role. I thought people would realise I'm boring! But, finally it was time. I sat down with this guy, Mike, and we worked out how we could make it work. We formed a whole new company called Fitness Corp, which is basically a holding company. We are both 50/50 shareholders in it. Fitness Corp leases my three gyms from me and his gym from him. He is the general manager of Fitness Corp, he runs it. He works to a budget, he makes sure all the leases are paid, he keeps the standards high and it works because he has a love of the industry and a financial interest in its success. We both make any major decisions like expenditure. If we were to take on a new venture, say another gym, then I would want to be involved. I like the creative side of the business. But, most of the everyday running of the business I leave to him now.

It's funny, from a Christian point of view I don't really like tarot cards. But before I had this business, way back when I was organising young wives social groups, we organised this lady to come and do a tarot reading for us. It was a bit of fun and we all went a long with our notepads to write down what she said. She turned over my cards and she said these are success cards, success in business. As she turned more over they all said success, success, success. At this stage of my life I was at home and not involved with any sort of business at all. I asked her what sort of business and she said 'I can't tell you, all I can say is that you will be very successful in business'. Then there was one card and she said 'you'll get to the stage where you think what am I doing? Why am I doing it? And, has it all been worthwhile?' I have had many of those times. I always felt that I could fail tomorrow. I never felt secure in my success. Looking back I still think a little bit of luck goes into being successful in business. I think you can be successful in business, or you can fail, and it's partly due to skill, partly timing, and a lot of it is due to financial factors.

I think it's a lot easier for a woman starting her own business these days. Attitudes are changing. Some men back then were really disgusting. I can remember buying a carpet once. I needed the best carpet for the least price, and I was trying to negotiate with a local carpet dealer. This man said to me 'I can get the price down more if I can get a massage'. So I said 'I'll find Lynn's book and see if she can fit you in'. (Lynn was our massage therapist.) He said 'I don't want Lynn to do it, I want you to'. I have never done a massage in my life and I was not going to start with that creep, even for a cheaper price! I was thinking 'I'm sure men don't have this problem!' So I told him to forget it and I bought my carpet elsewhere. Often when people see you as being vulnerable, they'll take advantage of you.

Another incident was with a local fashion store department manager who refused to pay me the agreed price for a fashion show. There was nothing wrong with the show, in fact the owner had sent me a gift voucher and a personal thank you for a job well done. But, when I went to pick up the cheque, the department manager said he was only paying me half the agreed price. He knew I needed the money to pay the models but as nothing was in writing I had to accept what was offered. All contracts were in writing from then on!

Even now, I still find some people's attitudes confusing. I've been married for four years and had the gyms for thirteen years, and yet if people want something they will go to my husband who has absolutely nothing to do with the gyms whatsoever. That hurts. My husband is excellent though. If there is any glory to be had, it often gets directed at him. He always steps aside and makes sure the credit goes to me. At the same time, if someone wants to complain about something, it's me they have to talk to. We like to keep business separate from our relationship, he has his business and I have mine. He's been in business for many years, so he's been able to teach me a lot.

My advice to other women is to do it completely differently to the way I did. Go into your business with an end or a goal in mind. My business has evolved. If I were to start another business now I would do a lot more market research. I think location is important, too. Also, do it well. When I started, I got away with having very little capital, and the industry I was in was just starting so customers didn't expect too much, but there aren't many businesses now where you can do that. You have to make a stand, be flash. Shout "I've arrived!" rather than just slip through the back door.

Nowadays women are going for it in business and I think that's fantastic! But they don't have to be tough. I like to think women can retain their vulnerability and femininity and still be successful. We don't have to become men to show our strengths, we should celebrate our differences.

Sheena Haywood

Sheena Haywood

SHEENA HAYWOOD PHOTOGRAPHY

Sheena Haywood started her career in photography as a cadet with The Herald. Her passion for snow had her photographing Winter Olympics while she was still a teenager, blasting into the world media arena. She came back to New Zealand with a reputation that snowballed into a successful freelance photography business. A decade on she delights in crazy projects and is well known amongst visiting and local celebrities. Recent highlights include being selected as an official Millennium photographer, photographing heads of state at APEC, and capturing the gruelling Iditarod Trail across Alaska.

I was involved in photography right from my school days, and I loved it, although I had actually planned to be a doctor. I started a cadetship with The Herald at seventeen years old, so fresh out of school I was a photographer. I did six years with The Herald including a solo year setting up the Rotorua office. This was an incredible time. 1987 was a huge news year. The day I arrived was the day of the Edgecumbe earthquake. The Rastafarians were burning Ruatoria and 5 year old Teresa McCormack was murdered that year. What an eye opener for a 21 year old. I then went to America to do my OE. My days at The Herald were an amazing training ground. It was tough, you didn't come back to the office until you had the shot.

I came back to New Zealand to work as a pool photographer at the Commonwealth Games. As soon as I arrived back in the country some people from the Press Club managed to track me down at my grandmother's house! I started taking photographs and people seemed to know me. I had no idea I had a reputation in New Zealand. It never occurred to me that winning press competitions and having my byline in the paper meant I was established. So it all happened pretty quickly. I was shooting pictures from the first week I was back in New Zealand. I had really intended to photograph the Commonwealth Games and then go back to America where I had an opportunity to work for one of the big newspapers in Los Angeles. But, I got busier and busier and that went by the wayside.

I was thrown into it and quickly had to figure out how to write an invoice, how much to charge and really start at the beginning. I asked a lot of questions, I was never afraid to ask. When you come back from overseas you have no money, so I was working part-time in a restaurant and living at my grandma's, trying to find my feet. I had all my camera equipment but photography is so expensive. I can remember thinking how can I possibly turn one roll of film into enough money to live off, as well as process the film and still satisfy the client? I got into a relationship at that time and Gary supported me wholeheartedly. He totally believed in me and gave me a push when I was wondering if I was crazy. Whenever I had any doubts he was always there telling me I could do it. So I did it. I drove around in my beat up Volkswagen, which had no security, with enough camera gear to buy a small house with. I just got on and did it. It was very scary when I first started, but I love photography and I love people, and people seemed to love me. I kept getting more and more work, and it snowballed quite quickly. That was eleven years ago.

Initially I was doing a lot of PR work. I worked for the city council, doing newsletters, brochures and community information. I worked for some of the hotels when they had VIP guests. And I did quite a bit of magazine work. Having worked for The Herald, some of the people crossed over between newspapers and magazines, so some people already knew me. And I already had a good rapport with a lot of celebrities that I'd photographed in my time at The Herald, so that flowed on into the magazines as well.

I can remember sitting in Gary's kitchen, writing my first invoice and trying to figure out GST. I didn't have a clue really. I rang other freelance photographers, and tried to gauge what was going on from what they would tell me. The sharing of ideas among other photographers was like trying to get blood out of a stone. Some of the key New Zealand photographers I talked to would tell me to go and ask someone else, usually international photographers based here. They tended to be fantastically helpful. Our guys like to keep everything to themselves. I was used to that coming from The Herald, where there's fifteen men who won't tell you anything. You learn the hard way. I just kept going. When people didn't want to tell me things I always managed to find out somehow. It wasn't a biggie really. The Herald was a huge training ground for me in dealing with social situations, in people skills as well as photography skills. If you can survive that, you can survive anything.

I kept waitressing part time for about six months. One morning I had an early meeting with a photographer I had huge respect for. He commented that I looked a little tired, which was probably because I'd been working until 2am! I told him I was waitressing and he said 'what are you doing that for? How can you put all your energies into being a photographer if you're busy being a waitress?' I thought I needed the money but he pointed out I was working for ten dollars an hour as a waitress, when I could be earning one hundred dollars an hour as a photographer. It wasn't until he pointed it out to me, I realised if I was committed to doing it, then I had to do it. About that time I phoned the restaurant, told them I wasn't coming back, and got on with being a photographer.

Sheena Haywood Photography stands for being available, being flexible, and coming up with the shot no matter what. I get some really interesting jobs, the kind most photographers would think 'how are we going to do that?' I get a lot of the curly jobs. I guess that's part of who I am as a photographer. An example is a shot I did for the New Zealand Millennium Book. They wanted a shot of a guy rap jumping down a building. To get the shot I had to go down the side of the building as well. The guy turned up in black. I thought we needed more colour so I gave him my bright orange shorts to wear. I didn't go down the side of the building in my knickers! I wore his shorts. That's the sort of thing I'm remembered for. I really aim to look after people so we get repeat business, and we do.

Another job I got to do for the book was in the reverse bungy on the waterfront. They put you in a seat, let you go and you go flying into the air. I wired up my camera and enrolled my flatmate and my brother in the project. They let us go, but because of the way the shutter operates on the camera, it kept jamming, so we'd have to come down, unjam it and try again. I did it at dusk, using a wide angle lens, because I wanted the lights of the city in the background and all our faces going aaahhhh! We had a lot of fun trying, but technically we couldn't make it work. I'm always borrowing my unsuspecting friends for photos, they never know what they'll be doing.

One of my passions is snow. I love the mountains. I was born and bred in Dunedin and my whole family are keen skiers. As I got more involved in my photography with The Herald, the boys would shoot rugby over the winter. My game was to get pictures published from the snow. I'd be up at the snow as often as possible, so I'd dream up shots that were newsworthy. Back in 1985-86, we were having really bad seasons. Lies were being told. Skifields were saying the snow was great and people would get up there to find it wasn't. I took shots of my friends standing around amongst ice and rocks and got them published. My name was mud within the industry, but it was the truth. Conversely, when it dumped, I'd rush down there and get shots of all the beautiful snow and get them published as well. It's swings and roundabouts.

Photographing snow is very difficult. You've got an enormous amount of light, you've got the cold to deal with, and you've got the physical aspect of lugging camera equipment around in that environment. Because the environment is very familiar to me, adding photography to it wasn't hard. Over the years I've fine tuned my ability to take pictures in the snow, but even now I don't get too cocky about it because of the light factor. It's so easy to overexpose your film. To get all the way back to Auckland, process it, and find out it's wrong is a major bummer.

I went to my first Winter Olympics in Calgary in 1988. I worked for the Associated Press, which was a mind blowing experience for me. I gained enormous insight into the world media from that. I went to the World Alpine Ski Championships in Colorado in 1989. And, in 1990, I went on a ski trip around North America, skiing 19 different skifields in 24 days.

When I came back to New Zealand in 1990, for the Commonwealth Games, I noticed the brochures and advertising for New Zealand ski areas used photos taken overseas. They had pine trees in them and clearly weren't New Zealand. I decided to take photos on particular mountains and started a campaign to educate the ski areas to use photos of their own mountain in their marketing. They weren't overly receptive because it was going to cost them. The reason they used these overseas photos was because they were free. It was a battle to convince them, but I went ahead and did it anyway. I went to clothing people and asked for nice ski gear to use. I had friends who were ski instructors, so I'd dress them up and take them out to shoot pictures. Then I'd go back and show them what I had. They'd say 'wow' and I'd tell them they can have it, but it will cost them something. It was always a battle, they'd try and fob you off with ski passes, but gradually it worked.

Snopix was born in 1990, a comprehensive photo library of alpine images. Snopix is part of what I do, part of Sheena Haywood Photography. I have six filing cabinets full of skiing pictures. When I'm old and grey, I'll have a great book on the history of New Zealand skiing. I had the ability to notice the lack of good snow photography and I went for it. That's changed completely now. People want the latest and greatest shots, which is great. But, with a lot of surfers snowboarding, snow photography in New Zealand has become a bit like surfing photography. They shoot pictures and give them away, so the New Zealand market has disintegrated. There's still a market for quality x factor images, though. A lot of my work sells internationally.

Every summer I do an offshore winter event to get a dose of the mountains. I get low altitude sickness very easily! I've covered four Winter Olympics now and I dream up all sorts of other things to go and do. Last summer I decided to go and do the Iditarod Race, a husky race across Alaska. Well that was easy for me to say, but really difficult to even find any information about. Then to figure out how to get there, and to come up with the money, it was like mission impossible. But, I really wanted to go, so I made the effort. I approached a lot of people and got some support with things like film, batteries and power bars. (I lost a lot of weight in Alaska!) I arrived in Anchorage and the next hurdle was actually getting to the trail. They don't look after the press. People don't generally go there to photograph it. It's an endurance race from hell. It's a hardcore, adventurous, extremely gruelling race. It's not designed for tourists, in fact it's not designed for anybody apart from the people racing on it. My mission was to find a pilot who would get me there. I spent a couple of days looking for one I could afford. Eventually I convinced Alaskan Air to take me along with a television crew that had hired them, for a minimal amount of money. I was totally at their mercy. The trail lasted nine days and they always wanted to be at the front of the race.

After a few days I asked them to leave me behind, so I was left to my own devices. It was real mystery stuff. I never knew where I'd end up, who with, where I'd find somewhere to sleep, what I'd find to eat. We went through tiny villages where the people are all related and there's nowhere to stay. They didn't have a youth hostel, or anything like that. I often ended up sleeping on the floor in someone's basement. It was all pretty basic. I couldn't even find anywhere to boil water to make a Continental cup of soup. I'd trudge around and eventually find something to eat. The temperatures were ridiculously cold. The coldest day was minus 42 degrees. The minute you walk outside you have to be fully protected, from head to toe.

Taking photos in that environment was interesting. In some villages I found people willing to take me out on their snow machines. All of a sudden you'd see a team of dogs come over a hill, you never know when they will show up, I'd stop the snow machine, and grab the camera. One day I made the mistake of taking my glove off. Within seconds I realised I didn't have my glove on. I took the photo, but then I couldn't stretch my hand out, it was locked frozen around the camera. It was so painful getting the blood flowing again, I was in agony. Even a thin little glove gives so much protection out there.

Each day on the Iditarod Trail was exciting and scary. I never knew what would happen on any given day. We flew through a lot of storms, I prayed a lot! Sometimes I'd be thinking 'what am I doing this for?' But it was fantastic as well, to be out in that wilderness. Part of my driving factor, and my motivation for snow photography, is being able to go to places other people couldn't get to and then being able to share those places and experiences. Most of these missions aren't commercially viable. They cost me thousands of dollars, plus lost income while I'm away. I get other things out of doing them. I like to be able to capture out of the way people and places. Often it's technically difficult. It pushes me photographically, to think about things I haven't experienced before. It's personally challenging.

My trips away often generate publicity for Sheena Haywood Photography. I put together a slide show when I got back from the Iditarod Trail and took it to schools, Rotary clubs, Probus. Woman's Weekly ran a story about me. The husky club booked me for their conference.

Self promotion is extremely important. It's hard, but you have to do it. You never have any money when you start in business. I'm not sure I have much more now! In the beginning I just gave my business card to everybody I met. The biggest marketing tool I had was talking to people. I'd tell them I'm a photographer, I love taking photos, and come up with ideas they maybe hadn't thought of. New Zealanders don't tend to take family photos. I love family photography and I don't think people do enough of it. Usually they get Uncle Tom to do it, who doesn't really know what he's doing, or Mum or Dad takes it and is missing from the photo. I don't market family photography but I do talk to people about photographing their children or their families. I'm getting much better at promoting myself. Now if someone tells me their daughter is coming home from overseas and they haven't seen them for years, or someone in their family is sick, I ask them if they'd like some special photos taken while they're here, if they'd like me to take some photos for them.   The best thing you can use to market yourself, is yourself. I am my best marketing tool.

I guess I've gathered momentum. I do yellow pages ads now and I do a photographer's portfolio, which features a page of examples of your work. Recently I've started sending out a newsletter called Exposure, showing snaps and snippets of what I've been doing. I've also got a website, this year. I'm working on developing it at the moment, so I can track who's looking at it, and making it so people can order images on line.

For about eight years now I've employed someone to help me at Sheena Haywood Photography. Usually it's in a backup role. That person looks after the phone, numbers prints, mounts and dispatches the images. There's a lot involved in taking photos. I have to meet the client, get the brief and actually take the photos. But then there's the lab processing, editing, dispatching. Somebody else can actually be doing that while I'm starting the next job. We joke about how the girls clean up after me.

Up until recently the people I've employed haven't been very qualified, so I haven't had to pay them huge amounts of money. I now have someone who's a lot more capable, but the business was ready for it, and we're able to generate more income because of it. Carole was actually my flatmate before she was my employee. I was getting so manically busy. She'd come home from work and say "what can I do to help so you can get some sleep?" She wasn't very happy in her job and my accountant thought the business could cope with it, so I took her on. It's working extremely well. Our relationship is on two levels. When it's work time, it's work time, and when it's home time, it's home time. I can be away shooting pictures all day now and know that things are happening at the office so I don't need to worry about them. On a Monday morning we create a list of what we're up for, for the week. By the end of the week there's usually a few ticks on it, we might have done half of it. You can plan what you want to accomplish, but there's always life coming at you at a thousand miles an hour, getting in the way of your plan.

I also employ other photographers sometimes. I'd like Sheena Haywood Photography to eventually be nationwide. I'd like when people think of a kind of image they want, to think of us. Sometimes they might request me, or they might use someone else from my team. I have a couple of photographers that shoot in a similar style to me, so when I'm busy I can get them in to do the work. For this type of work it's all about imagery, it doesn't really matter who took it. It is quite tricky to delegate photography to other photographers, especially while the company name is my own. I have thought about marketing Sheena Haywood Photography differently, so it's not under a human name, and could operate more as an agency. I have been delegating some of my photography now for about six years. As long as the client is looked after and delighted with the result, they don't always need me personally taking the photos.

Quality control is very important. Everything passes my eyes before it goes to the client. I'm now training Carole to do quality control as well.

Listening, and listening well, is a key thing in my business. Sometimes people ask for something, but it's not actually what they're really asking for. I really like to be available to people and where possible I'm the point of contact because it's me people need to talk to. If I'm really locked into a job, I'll divert the phone to Carole, but I really go for being fully available. I can take the mystery out of things for people, answer their questions, and hear what they're really asking. A lot of people are shy to ask about the cost. I'm always straight up about the money side of it, this is a service industry and you need to talk about that, so I give them options. A lot of people don't know what they want, so it's hard to quote, but there's nothing worse than people saying they'll look after you and then getting a huge surprise bill.

My rates are fairly flexible. Depending on what type of work it is, we do have set rates, but there is room for negotiation. I also do quite a bit of charity work, where I don't charge my normal rate. I usually charge them something to cover my costs and donate my time. People often have a budget and want to know what they can get for that amount of money. Nine times out of ten, people manage to push their budget up a bit, to get that bit extra.

I think a lot of women in business struggle with charging what they're worth. They're worth it, they've done the training, they're good at what they do, they often exceed the expectations of what they've been asked to do, and therefore they must charge for it. I still struggle with it, but I have wonderful people around me like Carole and my accountant Tim who constantly remind me I'm in business, not just out to make friends. Where I pitch myself is accessible. I'm in the middle bracket, middle to top. I find it better sometimes to tell people I'll get back to them when they ask me for a price. Once I know what they want, and can think the job through, I get back to them with a price. Otherwise you can end up kicking yourself when you get off the phone and realise the job's bigger than you thought.

I want to be financially free. Recently I wrote myself a post-dated cheque for two million dollars. I'd heard of someone else doing that. Really there's no reason why we couldn't earn that in a year. It's pinned on the wall so we can all see it. That's the goal. I chose two million dollars because one million is not enough, and more than two would be a bit greedy. So we'll see if we get there.

I have a fantastic accountant. I have an arrangement with Tim that I can call him anytime of the day or night with questions, or needing advice. If I get a curly job and I'm not sure how to price it, or I get a job that I'd love to do, and there's no budget for it, I can call him. There's a fine line between satisfying your creative juices and being commercial. I had to get smart, which isn't something you're born with, I had to learn it. I need to be sensible, I have a mortgage and wages to pay.

I also have a weekly business support meeting with a man I met on a course. We both have completely different businesses, Tony is a psychotherapist. We provide a support structure for each other. We talk about things that are bugging us or going wrong in our businesses. Then we talk about how we can deal with those things, and what sort of action we need to take. Then we check up on each other, and make sure we've done what we said we'd do. That time is safe and sacred. We both switch our phones off and are un-interruptible for that hour. It's amazing what we can achieve in that time.

I also have other structures in place to keep me on top of things. I have lunch with a group of professional women once a month. That's more life support, although business comes up as well. And I get great support from family and friends. They remind me to look after myself and take time out because I'm shocking at monitoring my own health and wellbeing. My health is a low priority for me, because I'm always so busy cramming so many things into my life. My friends and family know I'm busy, but I always tell them to ring me anyway. I fit them in whenever I'm not booked, or I diary them in so they've got a booked space. I tend to catch up with my family in strange places, usually on a mountain top somewhere.

When I broke up with Gary a few years ago, it was quite tough. He had been such a wonderful support for me, and I wondered where I would get that support from now that we weren't in a relationship. I had to get resourceful and find other means of support.

Although I would dearly love to be in a long term, intimate relationship, I realise it will take a special person that could allow my life to be this full. I've learnt a lot about what I do from past relationships. Having had a relationship with a person that didn't have a life, when I have such a full life, didn't work. It doesn't seem to work with people who have corporate jobs and finish at 5.30 every day, either. I think I'll have to meet someone who has as much on their plate as I do, but I'm not sure how we'll ever find time to meet each other! Small businesses tend to gobble you up, you think about them all the time. The only time I don't think about work is when I'm in the mountains. On a mountain top I don't think about the GST, or the bank manager, or the photo shoot on Wednesday. That time is truly mine.

I get a lot of young people contacting me wanting to be photographers.

Where possible I always get back to them and maybe have a coffee and a chat. I think the first thing is for them to sort out exactly what they want to do and why; you have to be clear in your head about what you want to achieve. There's a lot more training available these days, Polytech courses and even high school classes. When I was at school we didn't have photography. Although I must say I wouldn't be a photographer now if I wasn't allowed to be the spirited person I am, at Epsom Girls Grammar. They even put in a darkroom for me, so I could play. I'd often get locked in the art block because they'd forget I was there! So I have a chat with these girls and if they seem responsive and there's some work around, I get them to come and do a day with me.

My advice is 'hang onto your dreams, whatever they may be'. So many people will say it's impossible, ridiculous even, but I'm a big advocate for hanging on to whatever you believe in. That goes for anybody around me, but young women especially. There's so much choice now, you can do whatever you want to. My grandmother always tells me I'll make myself 'unavailable'. I'm successful, I'm single, I run my own business, own a house and a car. She thinks no man will want me because of all that. Times have changed. You are what you are and this is my life.

There are pluses and minuses being a woman in photography. I have been to the odd job where people have said 'you can't possibly be the photographer – you're a woman'. But, not recently. It often works to my advantage. I was an APEC photographer and met a lot of Heads of State. I photographed the Duke of Edinburgh, probably because I am a woman and could be softer, gentler. And I think women tend to be more intuitive and better at multi tasking. I can take in a room of people very quickly, see where people are, what they're doing and who I need to get shots of. Often I have to mingle within the group. Being a woman in that sense is an advantage I think. I always dress appropriately for the occasion and I never wear jeans on a job. I think New Zealand photographers get a bad rap for the way they dress. There's no need to be scruffy, I get quite embarrassed at the way some of my male colleagues dress. They stick out like a sore thumb, because they're dressed inappropriately at functions.

I don't miss out on much work because I'm a woman, but I've heard there have been times when people have asked others if I'm up for it, or tough enough for the assignment. Luckily I've had enough people on the inside barracking for me, making sure no one underestimates me just because I'm a woman. I hear about that through the grapevine, but I don't tend to make an issue of it. It's their issue, not mine. There are still some men in the workplace that haven't woken up.

Ten years down the track, I've made a name for myself, and I'm successful, but it's only the tip of the iceberg. My master plan is much bigger than this. Every morning when I wake up there's always so much to do. I have a lot of trouble sitting still and doing nothing. My vision is to build a House of Photography in New Zealand. I'd like to create a space with a late night café and a huge resource library full of inspiring photography. Photographers and creative people don't tend to sleep well at night. This will be a space where they can be nocturnal and exchange ideas over a coffee. It will also have a huge daylight studio, a fantastic lighting studio and darkrooms people can use. It will be a safe place where people can learn from each other, catering for all levels. People can get support here for their business or simple things like loading film into their camera. When visitors come to New Zealand it will be a place they can go to. Although I'll be a catalyst to make this happen, it won't be a Sheena Haywood project, it's much bigger than that.

For me personally, I'd like to move into the domain of making movies. I'd like to be a director of photography and make movies that excite and inspire people and leave them wanting to do great things with their lives. That is ultimately what I want to do. I think some of my far-fetched missions have been a background to allow me to move in that direction. So, there's a much bigger picture for Sheena Haywood. I'm nowhere near finished with this business, there's so much more I want to achieve.

The biggest piece of advice I have for other women is 'don't be afraid to ask questions'. Don't be afraid to not know something, ask. If somebody brushes you off and looks at you like you're a dumb blonde, go and ask somebody else. Seek out people who are supportive of you and what you're trying to do. Surround yourself with these people. Don't have people who don't believe in you. If the people close to you aren't sure about what you're doing, enrol them in it, show them who you are and that it's possible. My mum, although she loves me dearly, is still amazed I managed to make a business out of photography. She's a very strong woman, spunky and unstoppable, and I inherited those traits. She's a school teacher, and doesn't know a thing about business. I had to show her what I was doing and how it could work. That support is huge.

I guess there's still a part of our culture that says women should be looked after. The princess story is that young women will marry and somebody will look after them. I haven't done that. I've looked after me, and others around me. Don't wait for other people to look after you, you can go out there and do it yourself.

Judi
Sneddon

Judi Sneddon

BODY SANCTUM DAY SPA

A solo mother, Judi was down and out on the DPB when she first decided to embark on a career at the age of thirty five. With no money, but plenty of guts and determination, she's taken many calculated risks to get to where she is today —successfully operating two businesses.

I was born in South Africa, one of seven children. We were all encouraged to play sport and had very competitive natures. Coming from such a big family, you learn to fend for yourself. I definitely feel my family background helped to mould me into the person I am today.

When I finished high school, I didn't have a clue what I wanted to do with myself. In the end my parents considered what I was best at, mathematics, and decided for me. They put me into a company that trained accountants and that was my start to life. I spent three years there, which was good because I had no direction in my life and that gave me time to work out what I wanted to do. At the end of those three years I had a strong urge to travel. My boyfriend and I left South Africa and spent the next four years travelling around the world.

Four years later we were in Australia, and just about ready to go home, when we decided we were so close we should see New Zealand. We came to Queenstown and I loved it, but we only had six month tourist visas so eventually we had to leave. At home in South Africa, all I wanted to do was come back to Queenstown.

It was a couple of years before I made it back to New Zealand, this time with my sister. While I was in Australia I had trained as a massage therapist. I was working in a health food shop at the time. The opportunity came up and I thought 'that sounds like me'. Growing up in a big family, we were always massaging each other, it was just one of those things we did.

So we were back in Queenstown – what now? The ski season hadn't started yet, so I started advertising to do massage from home. At that time no-one was doing massage in Queenstown. Soon after that my sister and I both got jobs at Coronet Peak Ski Area. I loved Queenstown so much I didn't want to leave at the end of winter, so I got a job as a river surfing guide with a new company called Serious Fun.

I actually got my New Zealand residency through Serious Fun. They didn't have enough trained guides, so I joined them. I worked for seven years as a river surfing guide. During that time I had a baby. The man I was with at the time left as soon as he knew I was pregnant, so I was a solo mother from day one. I didn't want to work fulltime while my son was little so I did part-time river surfing in the summer and a bit of massage in the winter. But I made a pact with myself, when my son started school, I would start working fulltime.

It's amazing how opportunities open up in your life. The very month he started school, a friend of mine who had a massage business in the gym was leaving town. It was a natural progression, I took over from her. I had no money, I was down and out on the DPB. I started with just myself and one room. I called it Bodyworkx Massage Therapy. Within a year I built it up to a point where I had three or four extra staff and another room. I took risks and things worked out. I advertised to let people know I was there even though I had no money to pay for it. I was simply trusting that I would drum up enough business to be able to pay it off.

All I really had was a massage table. I bought all this advertising because I could put it on an account, I didn't have to pay for it straight away. I had brochures made. I just hoped that by the time the accounts started coming in, the work would be coming in too and I'd be able to pay the bills. The work did come in and I started slowly paying off my bills. I started with absolutely nothing, and from day one it went off like that. It progressed quite quickly. I built up my advertising and got quite well known in the major hotels. I built myself a good reputation. I had credibility and I really put myself on the line. I was on call twelve hours a day. If someone wanted a massage at 10pm, I'd be there when most other companies wouldn't. I think because of my reliability I got quite well known. Hotels started using me a lot so my business grew. Soon I couldn't handle all the work myself so I started to branch out and sub-contract some of my work to staff.

At that time I was still going overseas at least once a year. When I go overseas I enjoy being pampered, I'll get a massage every second day. I started to notice a trend in day spas. Everywhere I went I had my eyes open, researching trends and seeing what was happening in different places. I developed a passion to open a day spa in Queenstown.

I was back in Queenstown with this idea to open a day spa, but no money to do it, when I met an American woman. She's a massage therapist, in her 50's. She's been coming to Queenstown for her holidays and now she's bought an apartment here and is trying to emigrate. She liked to come and do a few massages while she was here just to keep her hand in. I didn't pay her, she just wanted to do it. She'd just arrived back in town when I was going back overseas. We started talking and I was telling her how I was ready to move on in my life and explore some new avenues. I told her I wanted to open a day spa, and she said that was exactly what she wanted to do. When I got back she was still in town and suggested we do something together. I didn't really want a partner, so I didn't take her up on the idea, but we agreed to keep in touch.

Shortly after she left, I found the perfect location. It was a house that was being used as a bed and breakfast. My son was playing there with his school friend. I went there to pick him up and I knew as soon as I walked in the door that it had a nice feeling. I knew I could do amazing things with it and from that moment I wanted that house no matter what. It was actually on the market but hadn't sold because of its high price tag. They were thinking about leasing it instead. I told them I was interested in leasing it for a day spa. They didn't think I'd be allowed to do that because of the zoning. There was a lot of red tape involved in getting permission to open a day spa there, but eventually I got through all the consents and applications.

The next problem was finding the money. I didn't have the money to do it. I tried the banks, but because I don't have a mortgage, they wouldn't lend me any money. I couldn't ask my family in South Africa for the money and there was no-one else who could lend it to me. The bottom line for me was to go into partnership with this woman. For me the benefit was financial, for her, investing in a New Zealand company would help her residency application. She kept emailing me and said 'Judi, do what you like but I am really interested in doing this with you'. In the end I realised this was the only way I could do it.

So we went in and invested a certain amount of money each. We were supposed to each put in $30,000. I had $15,000 saved. The banks wouldn't lend me any money so I applied for a credit card. I got a credit card with a $10,000 limit on it and another credit card with $5,000 on it. That made up the rest of my share of the money. I also took a lot of risks with paying things off. That is something I do, I buy it and worry about the money later. I did that a lot to set up this business. That is how I bought the spa and the sauna, and completely renovated the building. That's really worked for me. I bought a lot of things on a minimum deposit and then pay the rest off. That is how I've managed to start this business with a very minimal amount of money.

My partner is silent and still living overseas. I do everything, I run the business. Eventually she will work here, too.

I feel to get anywhere in life you first have to have the motivation, and secondly you have to be prepared to take risks. I have a crazy nature and an adrenalin addiction and I think that flows through me in business as well. I have always taken risks and it has always worked for me. That's not to say I take crazy risks, you have to believe it will work.

Opening this business was definitely a huge risk. I honestly had no idea how I was going to do it, I just did it. It's all gambles, playing with things. Although I didn't actually have the figures, the money, I played with it until it all fell into place. Every risk I have taken has worked out. I trusted that the business would roll on quickly so I could start paying things off, and it has.

Negotiating the rent was a good example of juggling things to fit. I was supposed to move into the house, because I couldn't afford to pay three lots of rent – for the day spa, the gym and my apartment. The day before I was to move in, they told me I couldn't live there because the regulations had changed with the change of ownership. I couldn't believe it, one week it was okay for people to live in the house and the next week it wasn't. I was stuck with nowhere to live. Luckily my sister was overseas so I moved in there for a while. Then I had to think what to do with the extra rooms. I decided to sublet two of the rooms to complementary businesses. I now have a hairdresser and an osteopath renting rooms within the day spa. Doing that has brought the rent down for me so I can afford to rent another place to live in. So it's all worked out, you just have to try different things until it does.

I now have two separate businesses. I'm self employed in Bodyworkx and the Body Sanctum Day Spa is a company with myself and a silent partner. I bounce off both businesses and send my staff to work at both. I am thinking about franchising day spas around New Zealand. I've been told this is one of the best day spas in the country and it's certainly not a multi million dollar spa!

The way I've set up this spa is quite unique. A lot of these places can be very clinical –white, white and white. I kept with the art deco style of the building. I wanted it to be a bit more upbeat. I have furnished it so it's quite homely and comfortable. When you walk in the door you feel like you're going there to be pampered, not for a treatment. It's a much softer feel than a clinic, and we have gentle music floating through the house. The location is great because it is close enough to walk from town and yet you feel like you're away from it all. And, the views are spectacular.

My initial idea was a gamble, but it was based on my own market research. Queenstown is getting busier and we have a lot of international tourists coming here. From my own travel, I realised Queenstown was a bit behind in the massage and beauty treatments we offer here. I mainly target the international market because they are already up with those trends. Also we have so many international events around us at the moment with America's Cup and the Olympics in Sydney. And, we have a lot of internationally based film crews in town. I looked at the trend, the market coming to town and I knew it would work. It was a bit of a gamble, but I did think it through.

I am very bad at budgets and I didn't do a proper business plan. I always do everything in my head, but I did write a bit of a budget down on a piece of paper. Basically I estimated what the rent would be, rates and insurance and came up with a rough idea of what I needed to start with. I thought I'd be able to pull it off through paying things off. I got a bit of a shock. Lots of companies wouldn't let me pay things off because I didn't have a mortgage. Credit is very hard to get in this country. I have a good credit rating but it was still hard to get things on buy now, pay later terms. The only way around that was I had to keep trying different companies until people said yes. I also put a lot of deposits on my credit cards, knowing I could pay it back later, even though it was a high interest rate. I didn't have any other choice. I did go through a finance company on one item, the spa.

I think advertising is really important, but you have to work out what works for you and what doesn't. I did an ad on Channel 5, which is a local TV station that plays in all the hotels. It was quite expensive but it worked really well. My brochure is probably my best form of advertising. I make sure all the hotels are continually stocked with my brochures and business cards. One of the hotels approached me to do cards in their hotel rooms and I get a lot of people from those, too. I don't do much newspaper advertising. I think it's expensive, especially for once a week. Radio hasn't worked very well for me either.

Professional advice has been very important in the setting up of Body Sanctum. Initially I wasn't going to seek any professional advice, because I couldn't afford it, but I followed my instinct and it's been vital. It's really important to get the correct things in place at the start. I needed to get a lawyer and an accountant. I really needed these professional people to guide me along the way. I would definitely recommend getting professional advice for things like leases, partnerships, and employment contracts. It's not always what you want to hear, but I do advise it. I'd never needed these people before I set up Body Sanctum. My lawyer drew up the lease for me and gave me some great advice. Originally I wasn't even going to have a lease, but I'm so glad I talked to him about it because he pointed out things I was totally ignorant about. He also helped me draw up the partnership agreement. I had a basic idea in my head, but he put it all on paper and got it signed by both parties, so everything is in black and white and we both know where we stand. He did employment contracts for me, which I haven't actually got my staff to sign yet, but it's really helpful to know everyone's rights –yours and theirs.

I find staff are the biggest headache of the whole business – it's like having extra children. I don't know if it's just massage therapists, but they're very quirky and you have to pamper to each one's different needs. Maybe I'm too motherly. They come in to work and no one wants to leave, they spend all day here. I've had to make a rule they can't come in unless they're working, otherwise they all hang out here! I do enjoy the staff I've got, though. They're an excellent bunch.

I've learned a lot about employing people. I used to just say 'great you can massage, come and work for me'. Now even if they have an excellent CV, it's really only when I've tried the actual massage itself that I know, that's the bottom line. Massage comes from within.

It's not something you can just learn, you have to have the touch, the feel and you have to want to do it. You can't always tell that on the surface, but once they're doing the massage I know. Now I have a much stricter procedure for hiring my staff. When I talk to someone on the phone, I ask them about their qualifications. I get them to bring these in, along with their work visas because that can be a real problem. I have a look over their CV, but the most important thing is getting a massage and a treatment from them and feeling their touch. Some people may not have as good a qualification on paper, but if they've got it I can tell straight away. That's how I employ my staff.

Because Queenstown is seasonal, my staffing levels fluctuate a bit. It seems to work itself out. I tend to minimise my actual employees and then have extra staff who work on contract and have other jobs, or who are employed for a period of time.

The biggest challenge is juggling the business with being a mum. Because I am a single mother my son looks to me for everything. The hardest part of him being at school is that at three o'clock when school finishes, I should be going home and having a normal life with him. But most massages are in the evening, so when he's coming home from school, that's normally when I have to go out and work. He has spent a lot of time with friends or my sister, especially while I've been setting up Body Sanctum. I make a point of taking weekends off, and that is our time together. When things calm down a bit, I hope to be able to finish earlier in the day and spend the rest of the night with him. He's seven and he has suffered quite a bit while I've been getting Body Sanctum off the ground.

I always promised myself I would give him the best five years before he went to school. I believe those are the most important years of a child's life, so I didn't work much then. I river surfed part time, which would take up three or four hours, some days. I also did part time massage, usually while he was asleep. So I did give him those five years. At my age, I've travelled, I've had a child, but I'm only just starting my career, so it's quite a late start. Now I'm giving my career priority and he's at an age where he understands a bit more and he realises that I work to support us both. He also knows that to have the things he wants, like a snowboard and river surfing gear, I have to work. We both love travelling and he's been to more countries than most adults have. He understands, although he would still rather have me than all those things.

I feel that by putting all my energy into setting this business up now, soon I will be able to step back from it and let it run itself. I'll eventually have key people in place. I'll have a duty manager, a receptionist that knows what's happening, capable staff, and I will work from 9 – 3 and then go home. My greater plan is to be with my son. I don't want him growing up thinking I was never there, that would kill me. We get on really well and have a great relationship, so I feel guilty when I have to work. He knows that, too and plays on my emotions, which makes me feel even worse. It has been very difficult, but I'm sure it will work itself out.

I've been through some tough times. Queenstown is an expensive place to live. Being a single mother, on the DPB, not having any money, hasn't been easy. In retrospect, I think tough times make you grow as a person. I think you learn in life from your challenges. Having a belief in God has helped me through the rough patches. I'm quite a spiritual person so sometimes when major hurdles come up, I just leave it in God's hands and move on. Things always work out in the end, always. And living in New Zealand you can't go too far wrong really. The government looks after you, and people help each other.

Starting this business is probably the biggest challenge I've had in my life. It was like having a baby. For months I was up all night figuring things out, I had no one to help me, I had to do it all on my own. I felt like I was in a painful contraction, waiting to give birth, so I could get some relief. Finally I gave birth to the business, but it was a struggle, it certainly wasn't an easy delivery!

I had the support of friends, but no one could really help me because it was all new, no one had set up a day spa. I have a girlfriend who is a key support person in my life. She is the mother of five children and she's always incredibly positive. I also respect my brother-in-law, especially in business decisions. Both of these support people are very honest with me. They don't mess around, they tell me things straight up.

I think the two most important things in starting a business are believing in yourself, and passion. Without passion there's no drive or motivation to get anywhere. And definitely, you have to take risks. Sometimes you fail, but you learn from your failures and it puts you in a better position the next time. Having a positive attitude has worked for me every time. We all have so much potential but so much of it is wasted because people either don't believe in themselves, or are just too relaxed. I feel there's a lot of opportunity in New Zealand for people who are motivated, because so many people are happy cruising along, doing whatever. The sky is the limit. People can do really well here if they've got that little bit extra, that x factor, that passion, and they're prepared to work hard.

I have a long term vision. Body Sanctum is a stepping stone to something greater. I have a section out in Gibbston Valley, where I eventually want to open a health retreat. I have bigger dreams. I want to have a short career life and semi retire in a few years time.

It's funny, I've had people approach me about all sorts of things since I started in business a couple of years ago. People seem to see me as this big successful businesswoman, but I don't see it like that at all. I'm just an average person who's tried really hard and accomplished something. Maybe they think I have a lot of money, but I don't. It just goes to show, you can create something from nothing, because I did. And I know I'll do well in the future, because I'm determined to.

Vivienne Speedy

Vivienne Speedy

PARTNERS IN TRAINING

Viv spent years in the corporate world before having the courage to branch out on her own. Doubting her own qualifications for years, she finally realised that travelling the world and years of experience was equivalent to any university degree. She is passionate about what she does and now thrives on helping others realise their potential through her training programmes.

I actually started my working life as a dental nurse – the stiff white uniform, the starched veil, the red cardigan! That didn't last long, they told me I was a square peg in a round hole! Dental nursing wasn't really me. Looking back though, that was really where my passion for training kicked off. One aspect of dental nursing was teaching the kids about dental health. I used to love that part of the job and bribe the other nurses so I could take their classes.

I remember trying to get into the personnel industry at the ripe old age of 19 and being told I needed to become 'street-wise'. Naïve to the core at the time, I didn't have a clue what that meant! I started to grow up after five years working within immigration. Liaising with international visitors, migrants, refugees, sports personnel and entertainers to New Zealand, my curiosity was aroused and I decided to take on the big wide world for myself. I went overseas for six months and didn't come back for seven years!

I travelled extensively for the first few years, and Scotland and Spain became my 'second homes'. I found I still had a yearning to get into the personnel industry and finally found a job in recruitment in the UK – I guess I must have finally become 'street-wise'! That really got me going. It gave me a real buzz to interview people and find the right roles for them. When I returned to New Zealand I continued consulting and then managed a recruitment consultancy in Auckland. For five years I loved the industry – the fast pace, the energy, the demands and challenges. But when the stockmarket crashed in the eighties, it got very 'dog eat dog'. For me it became very money based rather than people based.

I decided it was time for a bit of self-analysis. What did I enjoy? What did I do best? I'd always enjoyed coaching and training people and had a strong gut feeling that that was what I really wanted to do full time, so I started to quietly put the word out. Initially I got knocked back on several occasions because I didn't have the 'required qualifications or experience'. I eventually got offered a role as an Area Training Manager with one of my clients. Persistence and optimism had paid off.

I found that a lot of people, like myself, come from a background where early in their lives they've been put into categories. I felt that the school system had basically divided children into three boxes –

those who are going to excel, those who are going to be great at being mediocre, and those who are not going to get anywhere. I fell into the middle box. I'd always been a bit twitchy about that. I'd wished I'd gone on to do further study. My excuse was that it would bore me, but the reality was I thought I wouldn't pass. A lot of the people I was working with had also been put in the same box. I was determined to break out of it.

I thought "What can I do to make a real difference with these people and to actually give them skills they can use?" I took to the training role like a duck to water. I really enjoyed finding out what people wanted to learn, how they wanted to learn and being a catalyst to make that to happen. But, there's only so much you can do when you're working as a trainer within a company. After a couple of years, I needed to stretch myself and broaden my horizons within the training arena.

I was given a break to set up a training division within a major recruitment consultancy. It was a great opportunity. The learning curve was exciting, to start from scratch and design and facilitate training programmes. After doing that for three years I found I got the biggest buzz from facilitating people management workshops. It really excites my spirit to see others shift attitudes, stretch themselves, master new skills and grow.

For a long time I had a yearning to go out on my own but never had the courage to do it. People repeatedly said "Why don't you just go out and do this by yourself?" My own self-doubt was holding me back. I came up with every excuse in the book as to why it wouldn't work. I was scared.

But the drive kept getting stronger – there was a voice inside me saying "If I owned this business, what would I do to grow it given that I only had x hours in a week? What would it take from me? What would it look like?" My employer's focus was recruiting, mine was training. One large corporate kept actively encouraging me, advising me to "Just keep doing what you're doing. You've got the recipe right, you don't need to change a thing". That probably gave me the confidence to make the break. So one Sunday night in May of '95 – I remember it like it was yesterday - I made my decision – "I'm going to start my own business – contract training!"

It was a really 'spooky' decision. I'd had the security of corporate environments for so long. It came down to thinking, "what's the worst that could happen?" It felt a bit like jumping off the Harbour Bridge without a bungy cord! At the end of the day if it all fell over I could always get another job and start again. Once I realised that was the worst that could happen, I thought, "Right, let's just go for it – dare to risk, pull out all stops and make it happen!" I put my heart right out there and I still don't know whether it was the right time, good luck, or good management, but I fell on my feet. No, I do know. I was passionate, committed, and enthusiastic – I gave it my everything, and then some!

Actually getting started was quite scary. My sister was wonderful, sharing her own experiences as a freelancer. She also gave me a book on how to operate a business from home. But, me being a big picture person, I scanned through it once and thought "who cares what you're supposed to do, let's just do it!"

The first thing I wanted to do was to create an identity that was uniquely me. I went out with some friends and after several bottles of Chardonnay we came up with the name 'Partners in Training', complementing what I was looking to achieve. From there I had business cards and letterhead made – and Partners In Training was born! I started contacting people, and from then on there's been no looking back.

I initially contracted back to my former employer, so having some prospective clients gave me a headstart. I started off facilitating a small training programme and ended up coaching over a hundred different managers within the same company. I knew inside that I could do it, but I've always had a bit of a hang-up about not having any formal qualifications. I thought people would think less of me because I didn't have any pieces of paper saying I could do it. Ridiculous I know, but to a certain degree I still think about it sometimes and I'm sure it holds me back.

Although I do a lot of corporate training, it's nice to be out of the corporate rat race. I used to work long hours in other companies and think, "I'd really like to be rewarded for this". Now I am the company. Ironically I work longer hours, but that's about commitment. I'm a night person. That's when my creative juices really flow. Sometimes I'll be working 'til two or three in the morning and I don't even notice the time.

Working from home is very different from the corporate environment. I love it. I purposely invite clients here so they know the environment I'm living and working in. If it's sunny then we sit outside in the courtyard and the dress code is very casual. Many a time clients have changed into shorts and a T-shirt. It's amazing what you can achieve in a relaxed atmosphere. Being a night owl, clients know that if they ring me before 9am they are likely to get me in bed (unless I'm training and then I'm up early like everyone else). Videophones will be my downfall! Most clients are aware they get more sense out of me after 10am once I've had my morning caffeine fix!

If they phone me at night and I answer 'Partners in Training' they know I'm sitting in my office, if I answer 'hello' then I'm in the lounge. I very much believe in 'what you see is what you get'. When I first started this business I disciplined myself to still get up at 7am every morning as if

I was travelling to work. It was a total waste of time - it wasn't me at all. A key reason for working for myself was because I wanted to work my own hours, and work when I want to work, not when I don't. One of the joys of being your own boss is if you want a day off, you can take a day off! (Not that it happens very often). Flexibility is the name of the game – working weekdays and often weekends. My earliest start was 4am with shift workers – a real challenge, but what the client wants, the client gets!

Initially I think I had a perception that facilitators had a certain strict code of what to do in training, what was acceptable and what was expected – and I did what I thought was 'right'. I've changed quite a bit in my approach now. I take a lot more risks and in the last year or so have had the courage to do things totally differently – to do things in my own style, not to conform to perceived expectations. I have a lot more fun. For example, I tendered for quite a big project with a bus company. I don't like sales presentations at the best of times, so I thought I'd do something different. I purchased and 'signwrote' a few small toy buses and whizzed them across the boardroom table at the end of my presentation to the Board of Directors! Daring to be different and show a bit of spontaneity made an impact. I had let go the need to conform to formality – and at the end of the day that secured me the contract!

I've never had a boring day since I went out on my own. I really love what I do – it's part of me, of who I am. It was a huge risk at the time and I worried myself silly when I first left the security of the corporate world, but I truly believe if you commit yourself to being the best you can be, it will actually happen.

I learned not to worry about what other trainers are doing. I had to focus on what I wanted to do and establish my own niche. I wanted to create a difference. With my training programmes the actual training is only a small part of the picture. A much bigger portion of my time is spent on actual up-front needs analysis and on follow-up reviews to reinforce ongoing results.

I spend a lot of time in the companies at all levels, finding out what they really need, building a very open rapport and creating customised programmes for them.

I secured one contract with a company dealing in diggers and compactors. I turned up in jeans to be a 'lackey' for the afternoon. They had me cleaning earthmoving equipment, driving tractors and this little digger thing I later found out to be a 'Bobcat'. I'd never driven one of these things before in my life and even had to ask how to turn it on! There I was 'bunny hopping' around the yard, having an absolute hoot not caring whether or not I made a fool of myself, doing wheel stands every time I hit the brakes. I was so proud of myself when I managed to reverse this beast onto a trailer! I went home looking like a grease monkey BUT I earned credibility, I experienced their business and I had fun. I really took my 'pink hat' off and adopted my 'blue hat' that day! Getting involved at the grass roots of a company like that - and showing a bit of vulnerability - really brings it alive for me. By experiencing exactly what a company does hands-on I can customise a programme to suit their real needs. That's my point of difference.

Setting up Partners in Training didn't require a huge outlay. My most expensive item was a computer, which I still haven't made the time to learn how to drive properly! Initially I paid someone else to type up my programmes until I got up to speed. I explained to clients that I needed to make money before I could afford my computer. It was very much one step at a time. I started off with a tiny little table that I worked from. My clients would've been horrified to walk into my so-called office, so once I started to get some business rolling in I thought I'd better get some decent office furniture. I concentrated on the essentials rather than the 'nice to haves'. My mobile was, and still is my lifeline.

One thing I kick myself for not getting right from the outset was a decent office chair. It sounds pathetic, but at the time I thought anything over $100 was a waste of money. It's not when you're getting a sore neck! So that was a huge mistake asset wise – a tiny thing but it makes a huge difference. One other mistake I made was delaying getting email. I'm ashamed to say it but I only got it in 1999 – it would have saved so much time, energy and effort if I had got it years ago - another example of me dragging myself kicking and screaming into the 21st century!

I'm shocking at managing money – always have been and always will be. I tried to kid myself that I could do my books by myself and that I couldn't afford to pay someone else. The reality was I didn't like doing it, I wasn't good at it, so it was just false economy not to pay for them to be done.

I also get someone in once a week to clean my house. That takes away the pressure and also the distraction. I used to use it as a copout when I had work to do that was in the 'too-hard basket'. I'd think "I'll just go and do the housework". I've removed that excuse now.

I'm much better off in so many ways than when I was working for someone else. I think if you're passionate about what you do, you believe you are good at it, and you can produce the results people want, then you will enjoy life more – and make money.

I had a fair idea of what to charge people from my experience within the corporate world. Initially I was hesitant to raise 'the money thing'.

Now I place a much higher value on what I do. When I started I was pretty green around the gills. I never charged for all my time and expenses until my accountant pointed out to me that 57% of my income was actually covering expenses and that was far too high. Now I do. I went back to my clients and asked them for feedback on my rates. They were really good about telling me what I should be charging other companies! No one told me what to charge for regarding incidentals when I started.

I calculate my rate on the value I can provide to my client. If I could guarantee them $10,000 worth of value for a day's training, then I would charge them $10,000 – I wish! Seriously, my rates are pitched around the middle of the market. I know I provide value for money and hold myself accountable to deliver results. I stand behind my guarantee of value. I'm not motivated by money and I have really strong ethics. I'm in it because I have a passion for doing it and love to see my training making a difference to other people's lives. I see working with my clients as long-term partnerships – many of which have been with me since I started.

One thing I'm glad I set up right from the start was a 'Terms of Business' outlining my terms of payment, guarantees, conditions etc. Whenever I send out a proposal my terms automatically go with it. My terms are payable within seven days. It's important to be up front about payment when you're talking to a client - Don't avoid the issue. I always say "these are what my terms are, how do these fit with your company?" Many people fall into the trap of not sorting that side of it out and then they find themselves waiting months for their money. When I'm dealing with a large company, it's not coming out of their personal pockets. But, for my business, all my costs are being met by me. I pay up front for all my training materials, accommodation, flights up and down the country etc, so it's actually very important I get reimbursed in a timely way.

Over the last six years I've always received payment within seven days, apart from a couple of minor delays. I also put a guarantee of quality into the terms so if clients don't get results then I'll put the fee towards their next training. I stand behind what I do. I have never forfeited a fee.

Something I wish I'd done a lot earlier was to get written references from clients I've done work for, and participants. I have a lot of verbal referees but in my industry, people are looking for validation, an assurance, a guarantee of quality.

I've never done any advertising. All my work comes to me as repeat business or referrals from other clients. I have to admit, initially I didn't advertise because I was scared I'd make a fool of myself if my business didn't work out! I acknowledge that for some businesses, advertising may be essential. But for me, for the time being, word of mouth is a far more cost-effective means of advertising and it's also far more credible. A company won't refer you if they don't believe you can produce the results and if they do believe you can do it, you can really use that to your advantage. To that extent I'm still not even in the White or Yellow Pages.

One of the hardest things I find is saying "No" to people, turning down business. Usually it's because either I am unavailable, or the client can't tell me specifically what they want to achieve. I need to know in detail what they want to achieve so I can work towards that. You're only ever as good as your last training. If you start with a vague outcome to achieve, you will only get vague results. That will reflect on your reputation. I'm far more focussed and results driven now and that is more beneficial both to myself and to the company I'm working with.

My company is "Partners in Training". I see it as a partnership between the client company and myself and that's not a short-term thing.

I let them know when they approach me I'm looking for a long-term relationship, which is mutually beneficial. Usually companies respect you for that. I have some clients that I've referred on to other people for training for various reasons and they have come back to me. I suppose that's an issue of trust and honesty.

I made a promise to myself to spend a maximum of three days a week actually facilitating training programmes – I need to take time to re-charge my energy and also to prepare future work. Naturally I break this rule from time to time, but then rules are made to be broken aren't they? I'm working on it! Early on I'd cram everything in, saying "yes" to everyone, thinking, 'What if I don't get any work next week, or next month?' – that sort of approach nearly burned me out on more than a few occasions. Regular workflow is maintained by sustaining long-term relationships, by following up and keeping in touch with clients. Clients often ring and want something done yesterday, but sometimes you have to say "no". It's not in anyone's best interests to take work on that you can't prepare for thoroughly and do well because you are too busy.

I think it's really important to keep any personal issues away from your business. I went through a patch where I poured all my energy into fixing a personal situation. My mind was in other areas. It was like I was putting out vibes that I wasn't available; so no phone calls came in and work tailed off. I had let the problem become an obsession and take over. A good friend of mine gave me a wake up call and told me I was playing the victim. That was a turning point. All it took to get back on track was me being proactive on the phone. I called half a dozen clients and within a couple of weeks I was back in the running again.

I had a lucky run for a long time where every contract I tendered for, I got. Then I had two in a row that I didn't get. I was devastated with the first one. What had I done wrong? With the second one I knew I wasn't really qualified to do that particular training. The company wanted me to tender for it because I'd done a lot of other work for them. I gave it my best shot but it didn't faze me that I didn't get it. It was no disrespect to me, no doubting my ability - they just found someone more suitable for that particular job. I finally learned not to attach too much meaning to the outcome. I wish I'd learned that lesson a long time ago.

If something works - do it, if it doesn't - let it go. Focus on what you can control, don't waste energy on what you can't. Don't let it pull you down. And have the courage to follow up on things that don't go your way - I've rung GM's and asked what I could do differently next time around. Ask for feedback and act on it. Even if you don't like the feedback, don't throw it out – learn from it.

Working by yourself can get a bit lonely. I have several mentors I approach for feedback and advice. I have a great friend who comes from a professional business background. Whenever I have self-doubts, I can relate them to him and he drives me forward again. I find I need people like him around sometimes to keep the enthusiasm going when things are swamping me. He challenges me, too, so it's not all warm fuzzy stuff. I have another friend who also works for herself and we support each other in a lot of respects and bounce ideas around. She is full of energy and works at the speed of light. It really helps to be both supported and challenged by such inspirational people. My other mentor is actually a client. He is a GM of a big corporate and I asked him to help keep me on the right track. I felt a bit cheeky asking him, but I just came out with it and he was quite chuffed! It made him feel good that I had that much trust in him.

Something I think is really important in business is defining your values and working with people who share similar values. A friend of mine who develops marketing plans sat down with me a while ago to work out what makes my business successful. He said, "I know you think you just fly by the seat of your pants, but you've actually got some core foundations there. What values do you operate from?" When I thought about it, I realised Partnership is one, and Commitment another – the enthusiasm and willingness to do whatever it takes to get the results. They are two of the five key values that Partners in Training is based on. The other three are Integrity, Professionalism and Open Communication. Ultimately, it's all about respect and I am fiercely passionate about what I do.

Being successful in business is also about having fun and really enjoying yourself. The minute you lose that, I believe you should be gone. Another thing I find is that more often than not, I'm slightly nervous before I do a training session. I used to think it was a lack of confidence, but I now believe that's my edge – and if I ever lose that edge, it's time to move on.

Ultimately, what I really want to do is to work with kids so they can realise their true potential right from the word go and recognise that nothing is going to stop them except themselves. I want to take the same leadership and people skills I'm teaching CEO's and managers, into schools. I want to give children the tools to be able to create their own future, to be able to take themselves out of those three boxes they can too easily be put into at school. It's not floaty, ethereal stuff, and it's not rocket science either. It's simple practical skills in communication, confidence and leadership that young people can use to make things happen for themselves.

Travel was a big part of my past. The people I met and the experiences I had travelling through different countries, touching different cultures opened my eyes. In hindsight, I see it was equivalent to any university degree I could've got. My travels formed who I am now and gave me the confidence to be independent. That independence eventually gave me the courage to chase my own dreams. It gave me a different perspective on the world and made me realise I was capable of success. Basically, it was all up to me.

I finally fell into my niche in my early thirties. I was in my late thirties when I went into business for myself. If only I'd had the courage to do it years ago! When I look back I can see that training was always my destiny, but I didn't have the confidence to 'go for it'.

I have a passion and destiny to work with young people. To do this I am now ready to train others to help me. For a long time I didn't want to be more than a 'one-man-band', but now I'm ready for the business to grow. I am really excited at the prospect of coaching others to get the same buzz I do out of helping others to realise their potential.

Here's to being a catalyst for others (especially children) to create, chase and make their dreams happen. Here's to all us of making a difference.

Sarah
Elder

Sarah Elder

TENNESSEE BELLE

Sarah was only twenty years old when she bought her first business – a small florist shop needing an injection of new energy and enthusiasm. She has built the business up successfully and, after two years, relocated to bigger premises.

I have always had an ambition to do something for myself. I think it comes from my family background and the way I was brought up. When I left school I went straight into a hands-on job as a florist. I think it was probably the best way to learn the trade because it was real experience, learning on the job. I feel it was better than going to Polytech because I was trained in the business aspects of the shop as well as the plant side of it. It was similar to an apprenticeship, I sat exams in conjunction with my on the job training.

After three and a half years, I needed a break and thought it was time to do something different. I went overseas for a year, just for a change of scene really. But I knew floristry was where my heart was, and I would come back to it, either having my own business, or looking for a manageress position somewhere. While I was in the States, this shop in Queenstown came up for sale. My parents looked into it for me and it was all go from then.

In the beginning it was quite stressful for a number of reasons. The whole situation was new to me. I was in a new town and didn't know many people. Also, I had been out of floristry for just over a year. At the start, it was a one person shop, it was a bit run down and needed a fresh dose of enthusiasm. I had run a shop before, so I knew what an established business ran like, but it was a huge learning curve to get a business up and going. I wanted to see it succeed.

Being so young has had advantages and disadvantages. If I can do it now, then in five years if I feel I've done my time here, I can either move on and come back to it later, or go and start something completely different. Because I'm so young, the world is my oyster. I have plenty of time to do the things I want to do.

Financing the business was a bit tough. My parents were quite tied up and couldn't help out too much. I had saved when I was younger, because I knew I wanted to do something like this and I knew I'd need money to do it. A little bit came from personal loans. It wasn't actually a big cost to go into it, and I slowly built it up as I could afford to.

I saved a lot through looking at things really closely before spending money, and doing some market research of my own. There're always people coming in, wanting you to advertise and spend money on this and that, which can be quite stressful. I found it quite hard to say 'no' to people in the beginning, but I soon got more confident.

My parents have always had their own businesses, so they were a huge help to me with budgeting. The family I worked for in the States were also really good. The father was a financial advisor and he also taught business courses, so before I came home to New Zealand I did some of his night classes.

You really have to watch where your money is going. The main bulk of my business is in cut flowers and orders, so that's where I have to concentrate my energy, and make sure I'm spending my money on getting A1 product. Vases and things are sidelines, so I have to make sure I don't spend a lot of money on them, because I won't get a good return. Because I had managed a business like this before, I knew most of that. It was things like setting up the business and organisational skills that I found more difficult.

In the beginning, suppliers and wholesalers didn't have much faith in me, because I was so young. That made me strive even harder to prove them wrong. All the application forms require a date of birth, so most wholesalers refused to give me credit. I had to pay for everything before it was delivered. But within a month they could see I was serious. It was only a couple of wholesalers I had problems with, and I don't deal with those companies now because I remember what they were like to me. I would still be a good customer today if they hadn't treated me so unfairly.

When I first took on Tennessee Belle, there wasn't much business. I had to put my feelers out and find out who were going to be good clients, who wanted flowers on a weekly basis. I had flatmates who worked in big hotels, so I got contact names from them. One friend was involved in conference centres and wedding co-ordination, so I tapped into market information there. I got a good rapport going and found out their individual needs, likes and dislikes.

There was one other florist in competition with Tennessee Belle, as well as a couple of people doing flowers from home, so you have to be on your toes and supply the best product, with the best service, you possibly can. Between us and the other florist shop in town, there is healthy competition, but we also work in together and help each other out. If I run out of red roses and need a dozen straight away, I can ring the other florist, and the same applies to them.

All my staff have been wonderful. Because this is quite a transient town, it's hard to get staff that will be around for a while. I think it's important to have staff that clients can get to know and feel comfortable with. When I first took the business on, there was a fulltime staff member already. She was great because she was a local and knew quite a few people. She was quite creative and very good at what she did. But, she moved on.

I tried to find an experienced florist to take her place, but it was virtually impossible to get a qualified florist who was ready to go, had the extra spark I was looking for, and wanted to live here. I ended up taking on another junior who is in an apprenticeship position, so she'll be with me for three years. I enjoy having young people working in the shop because they bring in new ideas and they're keen to learn.

Sometimes it is difficult having staff that are near my own age. They sometimes forget I am the boss and not another staff member, which can be hard when I want them to do something, and I need it done right away. Also they can try to be my friend a bit too much, which makes working together hard, so, sometimes I just have to step back from them a bit. I get on well with my older staff. I have one lady who works part-time, and she's great, I wouldn't be without her. It's good having an older person in the shop for people to relate to. Often people come and ask to speak to the manager, looking straight at her, they get quite a shock when they find out it's me they need to speak to!

My staff are really supportive. Because it's my business I still feel quite guilty about having days off, I always feel I should be there. The staff are great, they always talk me into taking the time off, and promise to ring me if anything goes wrong. Then I feel I can go away without worrying.

One of the advantages of buying an existing business is the name is already out there. But you have to be really careful you know what you are buying into. Looking back, I probably should've done a bit more background research. I thought it was going to be easy, but the reality was a hard slog. You need to put the word out and find out what the locals think of the business. The locals are your bread and butter.

Usually you don't have to outlay as much money for the basic items you need. When I took over Tennessee Belle I took over the lease, which only had eighteen months left, so I didn't actually have to buy that. The stock list looked a lot on paper, but when we got there, it didn't seem like much at all. So I did have to spend money stocking up. There are so many things you need that you don't think about, tables, wrappings, things for window displays, stickers so people know where the flowers come from, cards. It all adds up, and it was quite a big cost.

There is usually some clientele that comes with an existing business. I probably paid too much for goodwill. That was something I should have looked into a little deeper. I didn't really need to do too much advertising, because people already knew Tennessee Belle was there, and they knew it was a florist. I advertised 'same place, different face', so people were aware the business was under new management. I had the occasional problem with people who didn't realise the business was being run by a different person. I actually feel like I have started this business myself. I have spent a lot of time and effort building the business up to what it is now.

When the lease expired I decided to move to a bigger shop. I had been thinking about moving for a while. Where I was the foot traffic wasn't good, but people knew I was there. The shop was too small and I wanted to expand. I didn't feel like I was doing as well as I could be in such a constricting environment. And, it was far too small to have three people working at once. We were getting titchy with each other. The previous florist I had worked in was huge and that was what I was used to, it took me ages to get used to working in such a confined space. The biggest drawcard with my new shop is the spaciousness.

The new building was quite expensive to start off with, but I managed to negotiate an arrangement that I could afford. I couldn't have made a better move. It's been wonderful for the business. Many locals thought it was a new florist in town, they didn't realise I had been around the corner for years! So it's brought in a lot more local business. Interflora has boomed as well with overseas visitors walking past. The shop is quite eye catching from the street and the smell is a huge drawcard. In the old shop we didn't get much business through foot traffic, we relied almost solely on telephone business. Now I try to have several ready made bunches of flowers at the door and they sell quite quickly.

As far as the shop layout goes, I didn't have the money in the beginning to do much with the first shop. Now I've been around for a while, and I've got a few more clues about what I'm doing, so it was the right time to expand. I wanted the shop to be eye catching from the road. I felt that blue would bring out the colours of the flowers. Because it is such a big space I could get away with such a dark colour. I tried to go for a Mediterranean look. I wanted the layout to be easy for people to walk around, with the flowers in the centre. I was on a tight budget, so Mum and Dad helped me out, building shelves and painting. We got an old sink from home and painted it up. It's not the most modern item in the shop, but it does the job and it looks authentic.

My family have been hugely supportive. In fact, when I took the business over, I couldn't get back to New Zealand for a couple of months. It was my parents who ran the shop until I got home. They were my backbone in the early days.

I didn't really use any professional advice until I moved into the new premises. I didn't know anything about leases, but my solicitor was really on the ball and he went over the new lease. I use an accountant now that I am busier. In the beginning I did the accounting myself, it was quite small and easygoing. Now it's not quite so manageable, I wouldn't be able to deal with it all myself.

There have been rough times. When I first started, I'd just got back from the States and I'd broken up with my boyfriend, so I was a mental wreck. I remember having a really bad day once, I'd just had a row with my ex-boyfriend on the phone, a customer walked in and I burst in to tears. I had to make up some excuse about some sad news from home. But that was the turning point. I decided I either had to be here and make a go of it, or ponder on what could have been. I decided to make a go of it.

Since then I've got more involved in the professional florist circle. I have taken on roles as the Secretary / Treasurer of Interflora and Secretary of the New Zealand Professional Florist Association. Being involved in these organizations gives my business a little bit more. People start recognising me and I've gained the support of other florists. When I have problems, I can go to these florists for advice. Some of them have been in the industry for twenty five, thirty years. These people have endless knowledge and I can learn so much from them. These are the people you need to surround yourself with, they boost your confidence.

After being in business for a couple of years I feel like I'm 35, not 22! But I have always related more easily to older people, and had a more mature outlook on life than most people my age. Most people are really supportive of me because they see me out there doing it, trying to make a go of it, and they respect that.

I went into this business as a five year venture, so I'm really putting all my effort into building it up as much as I can. When five years is up I'll review it, and maybe take a break.

There is so much you learn along the way in business, and most of it you learn just by getting in there and doing it yourself. You have to be positive and try and make the most of everything. Even negative feedback is an opportunity to make your business better. You build business by turning negatives into positives.

Ella Louise was born earlier this year, so life has become even more hectic! However my organisational skills have come a long way, which has actually helped me with the business as well. I juggle work and Ella quite efficiently now and at the moment her daily routine includes having a sleep at work during the day. When she gets a bit busier I may have to re-evaluate and find an alternative!

Having a family and running a business is always going to be a busy lifestyle. Having great staff and a supportive partner and family has made all the difference - it's helped me keep my sanity! I feel now that life is complete. If I could go back, I wouldn't make any changes. I feel satisfied with what I have and what I have made of things.

Annette
Milligan

Annette Milligan

THE INDEPENDENT NURSING PRACTICE

After dealing with a tragic personal loss, Annette decided to train as a nurse. A pioneer in independent nursing care, she set up The Independent Nursing Practice with two other nurses in 1989. In the wake of the stock market crash, and an era of free nursing care, they set up their practice against unfavourable odds. A decade on, Annette is the only remaining director. The practice is thriving, fulfilling clinical, educational and corporate roles in the community, and winning many business awards.

I think who you are, and where you've come from, your family upbringing, is a huge factor in your ability to succeed in business. I grew up in a family of seven children on a sheep farm near Tuatapere, Southland. We were raised to take on considerable responsibilities, and as a result of that grew up to be very independent and quite self-sufficient.

Another important background factor in my business is that I've had some personal tragedy in my life. When I was 26 I had a stillborn child that almost cost me my life as well. That was a complete catastrophe. I was seven months pregnant when my body started to fight the pregnancy. I went into hospital with extremely high blood pressure, failed kidneys, damaged liver, pretty much my whole body was a mess. Every test that could be abnormal was. At that stage the baby was alright. They transferred me from Invercargill hospital to Dunedin for dialysis. When I left Invercargill, the whole family was lined up, crying their hearts out, waving me off in the ambulance. Everyone was expecting me to die, but somehow, on the trip to Dunedin, I got a bit better. But, as I improved the baby's conditioned worsened. The baby was delivered by caesarean. Although I knew the baby wasn't well, I had a perception of a sick baby, not a dead baby. The baby was stillborn. That was such an atrocious year, 1981, and at no point did anyone suggest counselling to us. We were simply expected to struggle quietly on as best we could. That year was like an atomic bomb going off in my life; I lost my child, I lost my health, I lost my career in social work. By the end of the year I was physically a wreck and emotionally just holding on. It was also the beginning of the end of my marriage.

We came to Nelson and started to rebuild our lives. I was absolutely shattered. I slowly got my health together and got a job in a delicatessen. It wasn't long before I could see that wasn't very fulfilling. One day I had a flash of inspiration and decided to enrol in the three year nursing course. I found the nurses training really interesting, graduated and went on to work in Nelson hospital.

After a couple of years I was getting a bit bored, I obviously have a very low threshold for boredom! I nursed a woman who suggested I start an independent nursing practice. I didn't even know what that was at that stage. Later I went and had a long talk with her about it, but it just seemed far too hard.

It was about that time the scandal was exposed at National Women's. I followed that whole case really closely. After that I knew the health system was never going to be the same again. I went on a skiing holiday and was coming back when Sandra Coney's book, The Unfortunate Experiment, was released. I bought it, sat down in Christchurch airport and started reading. I read that book quite quickly, although sometimes I could only read a paragraph at a time. I felt like it was my story. I read and cried and read and cried some more. Afterwards I felt so much better, my story had been told, it was out there.

There was a series of exposes that year and it was Mary Griffith, who said 'that's it, I've had enough, I want to start a nursing practice'. Although I was actually planning to go to America, I knew in a millisecond that an independent nursing practice was where I was heading. I'm convinced the only reason I was in the space to pick the idea up was I'd finally dealt with the trauma that had happened earlier in my life. I feel it's absolutely crucial to deal with any personal issues you have before you start in business. Being in business is very demanding. You'll never make it if you're carrying around rubbish from the past. You've got to deal with your crappy marriage, or your crappy kids, or crappy whatever, first, so you can focus all your energies into the business. The timing was right for me. I'd been able to lay my ghosts from the past to rest.

Originally there were three of us that set up The Independent Nursing Practice, all trained nurses, Mary Griffith, Flavia Goulding and myself. We worked hard for about six months, working out how it would operate, how we could make it work. We upskilled ourselves clinically as well as learning business skills in a huge hurry. We also set up a very strong and enduring foundation for our partnership. Developing that partnership was very important for us.

We opened the doors on 13 February 1989. Our first appointment was booked within the first hour and we went from strength to strength from there. The three of us did everything, reception, paperwork, marketing, as well as the nursing. We drew no wages for the first 18 months, so we all worked at other jobs as well. We each put in one hundred dollars every month and subsidised that with our labour. We were grossly undercapitalised, but we didn't want to risk borrowing any money. That money paid for things like business cards and photocopying. When any extra bills came in we split them three ways.

At the time it was quite a new concept for people to have to pay for nursing services. People were used to receiving free nursing care. There were no precedents set at that time for paying nurses. So, we weren't just setting up a new business, we were creating a whole new role for nursing. We couldn't be sure how it would go.

We realised we would have to develop services people would be prepared to pay for. The obvious area for us to start with was sexual health. At the time there were no Family Planning or Sexually Transmitted Disease clinics in Nelson. It turned out to be a tremendous choice for us because people will always be having sex, always. They will always need contraception, it's an ongoing business.

We also do a lot of work in preventative care. We wanted to be able to give people information to be able to make their own choices about their healthcare. We realised there was a big role for us to play in education. I had a teaching background, I'd trained as a teacher before I went into social work. We soon developed a reputation as a teaching organization as well as offering clinical services. We were in the schools teaching sexual health almost from day one.

We worked so hard in those first few years. We had a lot of support from various people, including other nurses we worked with. They were great because sometimes we'd be burrowing so deep into a hole we couldn't see new opportunities. A good friend came to me one day and said 'Annette, you've got to look for where the money is, and it's not in this.' She told me about other people who were developing Access training courses – at least job training was being funded!

I knew we could offer great courses so I quickly shot an application off to the Department of Labour. One afternoon, a guardian angel wafted into the practice. I didn't know who she was, and I still don't, but she wafted in and said 'I've seen your proposal, and I think it's a fabulous concept, but you've written it in a way it will never be heard by the Labour Department'. She told us who to contact to ask for the proposal guidelines. She also said our pricing was ridiculously low, and we should pitch it between this and this. And then she wafted out again. That was amazing. She thought it was a great idea so she gave us the information we needed to get it off the ground.

We got the documents, rewrote it and repriced it. I wrote the proposal, wrote the curriculum and then taught most of it. I also got some other people in to help teach. It was six weeks of dawn to dusk, seven days a week. The people on the course got a lot out of it and it was good for us too. It was like breaking out of the square. It wasn't traditional nursing, but it was nursing, we were teaching wellness.

Teaching and running courses has gone on to be a big part of the nursing practice. We run courses in areas such as stress management, assertiveness, self esteem, menopause, giving up smoking, breast management. It's a major side of our business.

I worked seventy hours a week for the first two years. I didn't want to take time off because there was always something to do and I wanted so badly for it to work. But there was a point when I realised I was really tired. Although each day was extremely busy, I had enough insight into myself to realise that I had to stop, take a look at my life and change something. I looked around and realised my housework hadn't been done for months, so I got a housekeeper. And I had a day off. I thought about how often I needed to take a day off and I decided every three weeks. So I juggled the rosters to accommodate me having a day to myself every twenty one days. I identified the fact I was driving myself into the ground, and I wanted to last the long haul rather than burn out. You have to have a capacity to see what is realistic, to make it work. I could never go back to that now. I have strived for a sense of balance, and now I usually only work five days a week.

I think one of the main strengths of the business is it's never had a massive amount of government funding. Because the practice is a user-pays system, we are heavily client focussed. We give our clients the best treatment and the best information we can possibly offer. We want them to have a positive experience. If we don't give them that, they won't come back. Ultimately I've been able to get some contracts with the government, but it's only a minor part of the Practice income.

We did a survey before we started, asking people what sort of services they would use us for, and how much they would pay. The results from that survey were abysmal. People would pay nurses who had done three years of tertiary study $5-$10 an hour! And those were responses from mostly 30-50 year old, professional women. We took this to the accountant thinking it was never going to get off the ground. But we persevered and set our pricing at a level that met our needs. It seemed outrageous at the time, but we soon learned the cost of running a business.

Government legislation has huge effects on our business. Because our business is quite unusual, nobody thinks to include us in legislation. The introduction of community cards nearly destroyed our practice in one fell swoop. Our fee structure at the time was just covering what we needed, a set price for adults and a price for school students that we kept as low as possible. The introduction of the community services card meant we had to lower our fees for beneficiaries, but we couldn't claim the subsidy that doctors do. That meant a huge and sudden loss of income to the practice with no prior warning at all. We had the option of rolling with it or closing the doors.

That happens all the time. Once, in the course of 24 hours I heard three pieces of news via the media that would impact severely on our business. I've learnt to be very flexible, you have to be able to cut and run and deal with things without allowing them to completely wipe you out. I think the key to survival in business is to be able to take the knocks and bumps, to be able to bounce back. I often think of myself as the Incy Wincy Spider. Storms come and wash you away, destroying a lot of your hard work. You have to weather those storms and, when the sun comes out, be prepared to start all over again.

You've got to develop strategies for dealing with the unexpected. There's no point getting in a tizz about something, wasting energy, and having sleepless nights, you have to find some inner resilience. At one point I was literally on the verge of closing the doors and Flavia said to me, 'Annette, I can't go home to my four kids and say there's no dinner tonight because I haven't got any money to buy food, I have to think of some way to feed them. And it's the same here. We can't just close the doors because we haven't got any money. We have to think of a way to keep the doors open.' I come back to that all the time. When things get rough, you just have to think 'how am I going to make this work?'

I know how the systems work now, so I'm better equipped to deal with them. I actually have several contracts with the government at the moment, allowing me to provide certain services at a subsidised rate. But, I was never unhappy that we didn't get 100% funding from the government. Funding can be cut off in an instant. I feel we have security in the way this business has built and the fact that it is based on client satisfaction.

One of my risk management strategies is to keep income coming in from a variety of sources. I think that's a good survival mechanism. Having so many fingers in so many pies has allowed me to roll with sudden punches. There's been many times when one part of the business has fallen over, but I've been able to push another part of the business up to carry the loss. I don't like the vulnerability of specialisation. I don't ever want the majority of my income coming from one source, for me that's too risky.

It's also important to put your energies into the areas that are bringing in the income. I now have the ability to look at the whole picture and say 'that part has no value to the practice, should I get rid of it?' I might look at other parts and say 'that doesn't bring in much money but it's good for other reasons, so I'll keep it going but I won't put too much energy into it'. I look at new projects that have potential to generate a lot of income and put a lot of energy into those. It's really important to keep your eyes open to the future and not be wedded to things you've done in the past, just because you've it done before.

We do a lot of marketing and promotion, especially in the early days although we never had a lot of money to spend on it. Our advertising budget is bigger now, but it's still not huge. We've got a lot of media coverage and that's been free. We spent a lot of time writing magazine articles and we do radio programmes. I recorded about 900, one minute long, programmes on various health topics for the local radio station, which play every day. We actually got a radio award for the best information series for those. I think keeping your profile up is crucial - I put a lot of time and energy into keeping our name out there.

We've always had flyers and brochures and I now do a quarterly newsletter. Whenever I go to speak or take a course anywhere, I always take stacks of brochures and newsletters. I see all these people as marketing opportunities, they all know people who could use our services. Most of our marketing is done on the cheap, I make our word processor and our photocopier work really hard. Of course the most successful marketing is word of mouth. I concentrate on making the practice a place people want to come to. I want this place to be friendly and really nice. I make sure that our clients get a really good service and want to come back.

I realise I have to set boundaries within myself otherwise I'll burn out. My number one priority has to be myself. I have to do whatever I can to keep myself going. If I fall down in a screaming heap, the practice will go under too, it's as simple as that. So, if I'm working I give 100%, and if I'm relaxing it's 100%. I know I could spend every waking hour working on the practice, but I don't, I get out and do other things. Setting boundaries in the business has been crucial. I have to do things in my personal life that are just for me. I've just learnt to fly a plane. I try to make sure my partner's needs are being met, which in turn means my needs get looked after. My home is a bit like a refuge. It's calm, it's relaxed and Chris sees to it that my "zoom genes" as he calls them, are kept under a bit of control. I've seen too many people burn out – it's good for me to be with someone who slows me down.

One thing I've been doing for the last couple of years is having professional supervision. I see a psychologist once a month and that is my debriefing time. That is the best thing I can do to keep my head in order. This is a safe place where I can work out anything that's bothering me. I've found this supervision is the most valuable tool I have for working through issues.

I've been the sole director in the practice for several years now. I actually really enjoy it because I've created a job that's constantly changing and evolving. I still have some clinical time and do some of the teaching, but I'm gradually passing that on to others. I just love running the business side of it. I love the excitement and the opportunities and I like creating new projects. I'm much better at starting things off than maintaining them, and a lot of nurses are much better at maintaining things once they're started so it's a perfect combination. I get projects up and running and then I hand them over and look for new things. It's not always easy to hand over your pet projects but I always want to start something new. You can't do everything without burning out, so something has to go.

I would consider taking on another business partner, if the right person came along. But, I'm very nervous about it. I'm a bit of a lone wolf, really, I like my own company. It worked with Flavia because we knew each other so well, we knew each other's needs. This business is my baby — I've put my heart and soul into it for over a decade now. I don't want someone stepping in and having everything turn to custard. I've seen other businesses hit the wall because of terrible partnerships. I would much rather have the odd sleepless night worrying how I'm going to pay the GST, than worrying how the hell am I going to get out of this heinous business partnership! Be very careful who you go into business with.

Planning is very important to me. I take a day out every year when I do nothing but plan. We've always done that. In the early days, we did it as a group with an outside facilitator. The facilitator helped us to work through any issues and move forward. Now I just do it myself with lots of pieces of paper spread all over the floor and a felt tip pen. I usually do that about October / November and then every month I spend some time checking on my progress and looking back to the overall plan.

Part of my planning involves finances. I'm fanatical about cashflows. I have a loving relationship with my bank and I stay in fairly close contact with the bank people. I do my cashflows monthly and keep the bank informed. That way they don't get any surprises and they always cover my overdraft.

I don't think the business skills you need are as difficult as people make out. I was involved in setting up a gallery where I learnt the basics like setting up a cash book, doing GST, employing people, PAYE. I was also married to an accountant. I thought I should do a business course, and my accountant said 'what for? Annette, you could teach this stuff, you've been doing it for years'. I think it's easy to be overwhelmed by the thought of all these complex business skills, but it's really not that difficult. It's like learning anything, it's just another skill, it's certainly less complicated than learning to read. The harder skills are developing a sense of your own values in business.

I've heard a rule in business that you lose money in the first year, you break even in the second, and you make money in the third. I don't think that's true. It's taken me ten years to reach the salary I was on before I started. It's been a long, hard slog to get there. Having said that, I also know that money doesn't drive me. I need personal rewards. I need an interesting job, I need control over my life, I need to feel that what I'm doing is a good and worthy thing to be doing. Because I can't have a child, I need to feel that I'm going to leave this world having made some kind of contribution. The Independent Nursing Practice gives me all of those things - it gives me personal satisfaction.

And now I've put in the hard years. I'm moving towards a greater quality of life for myself. The business is growing up. I have a wonderful team that can run it without me. I've got terrific systems in place and it doesn't need me so much anymore. I also have a wonderful sense of pride in what we've started. This business was pioneering stuff. I think we've created something that has advanced the course of nursing and provided more opportunities for women through nursing. Sometimes I walk through here when everyone has gone home, and I know everything in here we've built absolutely from scratch. I derive an enormous sense of pride from that.

I think it's important for businesswomen to retain their feminine qualities. There are times when I've had to be really tough, but I don't ever want to lose the warmth and caring that is my female and my nursing side. I don't feel women need to let go of their humanity and compassion in order to be successful. Women are sensible and good managers. Those basic things are instinctive in women and are fundamental in business. Women need to learn not to be intimidated by the problems they will face and to set realistic expectations. And, ultimately, you've got to have the passion to keep going.

Claudia Agusto

Claudia Agusto

Born in Chile, Claudia grew up in Australia, and now lives in Christchurch. Now in her late twenties, she recently set up Loyalty clothing / gallery with the help of a grant from Work and Income New Zealand, aimed at helping unemployed people get started in business.

I have always loved shopping, especially rummaging around in second hand stores. I'd find all sorts of amazing clothes, so I guess I've always figured it wouldn't be too difficult to set up a store with a secondhand clothing angle. I thought my ideal would be to go into an uncluttered shop and find beautiful clothing that wasn't too expensive.

My background has always been retail and customer service. I thought it would be cool to own my own shop and see what I could do with it. I guess I started building castles in the air with my own ideal in mind about two years ago, and it manifested from there.

I did my first waitressing job at The Globe, on High Street. I made tons of contacts there because I was on the front counter, so I was always talking to people. I told heaps of people about my concept and I was always encouraged so the idea developed quite rapidly.

I had absolutely no money so I approached the Canterbury Business Development Board about getting some funding. I found that there was no way I could get any assistance unless I was unemployed and had been for over six months – that was the bottom line. I thought that was really unfair. Here I was working my arse off, nine hours a day, five or six days a week, and I couldn't get any help, while someone who was sitting at home watching videos all day can get this money from the government. I tried every avenue but found nothing.

As it happened, my hours were cut back at The Globe, so I was able to register as unemployed and continue doing my part-time hours at the café. Once registered, I was able to do a Small Business course organised by WINZ. The course was amazing. In my head I'd gone through the running of the shop as far as the clothes go, the layout, what it would look like. But I didn't know the first thing about running the business side of it. They taught me all about the bookwork side of it, all the things that are essential to running a business, but aren't the fun bits. We did stress management – some people can't deal with the stress of running a business. Me – I'm stressed because I'm not stressed! We learnt about market research and how to write up a business proposal.

I think a lot of my market research was done while I was at working at the café. My shop was always going to be in High Street, never anywhere else. This area is blossoming. At the café I could watch the people coming down this end of town. I could see who they were, what they wore, what their careers were, what they were into. We'd get everything from poets to the Mayor of Christchurch, and everything in between. I also sat in a shop down the road for a while and just observed people.

The beauty of High Street is that it is such a funky environment, and I wanted to reflect that. I wanted to create something that would fill the gap, and cater to everybody across a broad spectrum, from an artist living on the bones of their bum, to a wealthy professional. I wanted it to be a non-judgemental environment so that it didn't matter who you are, or what your position is, you'd find something you like and enjoy the whole experience. Quite often you walk into a beautiful boutique and feel intimidated. I wanted my store to be as far away from that as possible, and still be beautiful.

To be considered for a grant, you have to put forward a business proposal. WINZ and the Small Business Centre work in together. Basically, the business centre provides all the business information and support, and WINZ hands out the money on their recommendation. The business centre then monitors your progress, so if you fail, they pull the plug on your funding.

My first business proposal failed and I bawled my eyes out because I'd worked so hard. Basically it was just lacking. The business proposal has to be quite detailed. It's a plan, starting with your idea, detailing your market research, and showing capital, costings, and revenue. It's pretty outrageous really because how can you tell how much you're going to sell? But, you just look at your market research and from that assume what you think might be realistic. They gave me a report stating what was lacking in the plan and what was strong. I only had one strength, the location, which wasn't very encouraging.

It took me two days to get back on the horse, I was so miserable. Then I thought I have got to do this, so I got back on the computer, and I tried to improve the areas I was obviously weak in. I handed in my second proposal and got it back in two days. So it only took a week from the first proposal to the second proposal, which was really good.

They accepted the second proposal. In the first proposal I hadn't addressed certain issues and I needed to reassure them that I knew what I was talking about. They were things that I knew in my mind, but I hadn't been able to express on paper. They were really helpful and said you need to do this and this in order for us to know and understand your plan. I had to go through it with a fine tooth comb and make sure everything that was in my head was down on paper, so they could see it. It was one of the hardest things I've ever done. It's actually great that it's all down on paper, because now I can go back to it.

In that time I had found a location, although I wasn't sure whether to take it because it was upstairs. I had been telling everyone that I was looking for something to rent in the area. I'd been looking for ages when a guy that I'd worked with at The Globe came in and said he'd seen a place for lease. I went and had a look at it from the road and thought, upstairs… It was really drawing me there. So I got the guy to show me it and as soon as I walked in I knew that it was good. When I saw the space, I thought of a gallery straight away, and that was what inspired me more than anything to go ahead with it. Everyone told me not to go upstairs, that I'd be shooting myself in the foot. I thought 'narrow-minded Christchurch, open up a bit'. I took a couple of friends up there and they were encouraging, they gave me a bit of a nudge so I could feel completely good about it, a bit more assured.

The tutors at the Business Centre advised me not to go upstairs. They told me retail upstairs just doesn't work. But I felt that High Street was ready for it. Some of the funkiest stores are upstairs and it doesn't faze anybody. If the shop is good enough, people will go up there, a few stairs won't stop them. The foot traffic factor doesn't bother me either, because I believe in myself and I believe that my clientele will be loyal. I decided to go ahead with it. I received a grant from Work and Income New Zealand of $4,000 as capital and made do with it.

It took about a month for the grant to come through. The landlord was nice enough to give me three months free rent if I did the place up. It was a dive, a dirty, revolting shambles, rotting wallpaper everywhere. But I was so excited and amped I thought I could at least get in there and start cleaning while I was waiting for the money to come through. It was really helpful that he let me have that rent-free period. I got in there, cleaned, and when the money came through, I started spending it. I made $4,000 go a long way. To me it's about creativity, and it's a question of using what you've got and making the most of it.

I was fortunate in that I know quite a few people around Christchurch. It came in really handy that these people knew and liked me. I didn't realise it at the time, but I was always nice to them and in turn it came back to me. I got good deals on paint and things, and I had some good friends help me. I got stuck in there, doing the hard labour for two months, and did the place up. It was pretty hard out, and I was still working at the café part-time.

If I had known the amount of work I was about to do, and the hours I was going to put into doing the place up, I probably wouldn't have taken it. I lost twelve kilos running up and down ladders, painting. It was very rewarding, though. The location was just meant to be.

In that time, I had a lot of support from friends. There were two guys who physically helped me a lot. They put in a lot of hours, doing handyman stuff that I found difficult. People helped me in different ways. Some gave me lots of hugs and 'good on you's'. Other friends did things like cooking me dinner and even doing my washing. They were a tremendous support. It was hard receiving help. It's hard to ask for help but there were times when I just had to, because I thought ' I can't do this'. You feel weak in a sense, like you're giving your power away by asking for help, but I think it's actually empowering.

About a month into it I thought it was time to start thinking about an opening date. I was starting to peak, wondering how I could possibly do everything in that timeframe. In all honesty, even at the time I decided the opening date, I didn't have a clear vision of what Loyalty was going to look like. I knew what I wanted. I knew I wanted it to be minimal and beautiful. I knew I wanted the concept to be a balance between masculine and feminine. But it basically happened by itself. I would do certain things and then I'd get something else and it would just fit perfectly. It was creating itself and I can't stress that enough. People tell me 'it's so amazing, you've done so well' and I say 'Cheers, but it did it itself'.

I had to put the opening date back a week because I was nowhere near ready. The last week was intense. I was doing fifteen to seventeen hour days, going really hard, doing most of it alone.

I got the stock together in the last few days before I opened. The opening was at 4pm on a Saturday afternoon and I was still running around collecting stock that morning. Enough people knew about it and knew that I needed the stock there by that time so I had lots of support. I had promised myself that I would be in the shower drinking bubbly by 2pm. I didn't want to be racing around, spinning out. And that's exactly what happened. Everything fell into place.

A big part of the reason I chose this space is the gallery side of Loyalty. One of my greatest passions is art, all types, performing, poetry, film, mime... I wanted to share this space with local talent. It's such a big space and nothing is fixed so I can move things around and invite local artists to come in and do whatever they do. I don't charge any commission rates, it's just an opportunity to put something back into the community. And it's a form of advertising. So far I've had a theatre group in here – some friends of mine from Wellington, and an exhibition of torso sculptures made out of wire and plaster. It's happening a lot faster than I thought it would, it's just taken off on its own. I hope that eventually Loyalty will be known as a clothing store during the day, but also a place where artists, that don't have much money, can come and do their thing and share their art with other people. I feel really good about that and it's such an amazing space, the light is fantastic. I think it will work really well.

The opening night was an incredible success. There were people coming in and out all night. We were there until one o'clock in the morning! I was able to bring in artists, we had jazz musicians from the jazz school, and a mime artist who did an amazing robotic act. I made quite an effort to make it visually exciting for people, with things like projections on the walls.

The opening turned out to be the best form of advertising. I invited everyone I knew, including a lot of people I had met while I was working at The Globe. There must have been about three hundred people come through, from all walks of life, many of them customers from the café who've been really supportive. There was such a mixture of people and everyone was really happy and buzzing. It filled my space with an amazing energy, which has stayed in there. When you walk up there you feel all this nice goodness.

Apart from buying one ad, which I didn't get any response from, I haven't done any other advertising. Word of mouth works best for me. Whenever someone comes up here they always say someone has told them about Loyalty. I have always been into communicating with people about what I was doing. I was always talking to people, and now people just seem to know.

The initial intention was to go rummaging for my stock, but I just don't get time. Between nine o'clock and ten thirty when I open, I run around doing banking and that sort of thing. I have a part-timer who comes in on Saturdays, but so far I've been catching up on all the sleep I missed out on when I was setting it up.

There are other secondhand designer clothing stores in town, it's not a completely new concept. The difference with Loyalty is it's more like a gallery. It's clean and spacious and quite stylish. I have been very fortunate in that stock seems to come to me. Again, I use contacts I made working at the café. I used to work in a fashion boutique, and the girls that work in there bring their clothes in to me. Their turnover in clothes is quite high, they have to look good all the time, and you get sick of your clothes very quickly. I find that, too. I wear something a few times and then I put it out on the racks. I have been networking with all the girls in the stylish, high fashion clothing stores.

I also support the designers at the Polytech fashion school. Because they're young artists I take less commission from them. They put garments in and are so pleased to get some money because they're struggling students. And they're excited to have their work in the marketplace, and people seeing their label. It works for everyone. I get fresh, funky designs from up and coming designers, plus they're a good marketing tool for me.

I try and keep within my backyard and stay in Christchurch. There's really no need for me to look for national designers, there's plenty of talent locally. It's good quality and it fits with the second hand clothing really well.

I think the biggest lesson I've learned through this whole experience of setting up a business is that you can achieve anything you set your mind to, as long as you are passionate about it and believe in yourself. Nothing really bad can come of it. I'm going to die one day and I won't be taking anything with me. If this business folded in a years time, so what. I have learned so much in the past months about myself, about people, about my own strengths and weaknesses. That is invaluable. If the business goes under, and I don't think it's going to, but if it does, my ego will be bruised, but I'm not going to die, no one will be hurt, Christchurch won't fall apart. The worst that can happen is really not that bad.

And it's a mind set thing. If you expect the best, you'll often get it. Your attitude will take you to exactly where you want to go. If you know you can succeed, you will succeed, there's no other way – your mind creates your reality.

I'm not too stressed about Loyalty. Everybody I speak to seems to think I should be stressed every day! I don't feel you need to put any added pressure on yourself. What is the point of having Loyalty if I'm not enjoying it? The reason I'm doing it is so I can have a lifestyle and be in good spirit. If I stop having fun it will be time to give it away and move on to something new.

For me, working for myself is the ultimate as far as careers go. Not having to answer to people, or have someone above you nagging at you to do things. The idea of getting up in the morning and planning your day around what you want to do is the beauty of being self employed.

I always knew that before I was thirty I would have one of three things – a baby, a house, or my own business. Now I have one of those things, a business. Loyalty is just like a wee baby at the moment. I gave birth to it, and now I have to nurture it and look after it. And it's a challenge. I have to keep people interested and rely on myself to create an income. That reality does hardens you up a bit, but I think that's a good thing.

The most important thing is to believe in your idea. Don't worry too much about what other people say – you can take in their suggestions, but filter them. Take what you need and let the rest go. Don't be influenced by anything other than what you believe inside. Belief is essential to get where you want to be – it gives you strength.

Jeni Pearce

Jeni Pearce

**JENI PEARCE AND ASSOCIATES
HEALTH AND SPORTS DIETITIANS**

Jeni Pearce was one of the first dietitians in New Zealand to set up a full time private practice. Fifteen years later, she's fully independent, has earned a worldwide reputation and works with many New Zealand and internationally acclaimed sports people and teams. She's written nine books and is often asked to comment on nutritional issues in the media. Jeni's worked hard to get to where she is today - it's been a long, hard road to success.

Becoming a health and sports dietitian was originally a very unusual choice, and I think it just evolved. In the third form at Otumoetai College, in Tauranga, I knew I wanted to go to university to study something that involved food, health and people, but not to become a chef, a teacher, a waitress, or a nurse. The school guidance counsellor researched for almost two years to find the Home Science degree at Otago University. (This degree is now called Consumer and Applied Science.) As a teenager I had a vague, blurred vision of what I wanted to do, but no idea how to get there.

Going to Otago University was a shock as just about my entire seventh form went to Waikato University. I arrived in Dunedin, a long way from home, not knowing a soul and feeling very alone. My parents thought I had gone to the end of the earth! They have at times found my choice of lifestyle and the length and depth of study difficult to understand. They have been concerned regarding the insecurity of my chosen profession, the amount of time spent in tertiary education (seven years) and the long hours I work. It's been difficult for them to explain to their friends what I do when their children have chosen more typical occupations.

The degree involved a lot more than I initially expected. The majority of the subjects were science based and included food chemistry, microbiology, anatomy, physiology and biochemistry as well as nutrition. Clothing, design and art history were also incorporated. I worked hard and did well at university and graduated knowing I had two career options; work as a dietitian or teach. I remember discussing this with one of my lecturers and explaining 'I want to do both'. Her advice was 'no one says you can't do it all'. This has been one of my major life philosophies ever since. Just because no one has done this before, there's no reason why you can't. It's hard work trying to do it all, but it can be done.

I returned to Auckland for a year to complete my teacher training, but realised about halfway through this wasn't really what I wanted as a fulltime career. I stayed to complete the training which was extremely helpful with the lecturing and public speaking that was to come later. The following year I was accepted to train for Post Graduate studies in dietetics at Christchurch Hospital. After a very comprehensive year completing my dietetics training I began work as a dietitian in hospitals throughout New Zealand. This was a fantastic time and I gained a lot of clinical and management experience very early. Eventually though, I began to feel I was like an ambulance at the bottom of a cliff. I was helping to get people out of hospital, but I wanted to stop them getting there in the first place. At this time I applied for a scholarship to study a Masters degree in America for two years, not thinking I would ever be accepted. Six weeks later I was on a plane to Iowa State University. It all came as a bit of a shock.

Life in the USA was an incredible learning experience. I don't believe I would have had the courage to follow my career path had I remained in New Zealand. The degree was hard work, long hours, but incredibly rewarding. On returning to New Zealand I realised I couldn't go back to working in a government institution, but I still wanted to be a dietitian. The only way I could continue my career and not be based in a hospital was to work privately. When I explained to my friends and colleagues I was going to specialise in sports nutrition they thought I was completely mad. It just wasn't heard of as a career. At the time I think there were three private dietitians in the whole country. This was one situation where I just decided I would make it work. I didn't care what it cost me, I was going to make it happen.

In the meantime I needed to be creative to support myself financially. I taught chefs, worked in universities and lectured at polytechnics, while I built my private practice. Today I am completely independent as a private practice dietitian. It has taken fifteen years since arriving back in New Zealand to get to this stage.

Returning from America I headed to Hamilton. 'Why Hamilton?' people often ask. I came back to a town where I knew only one person, for a relationship that quickly disintegrated. I had changed significantly over the two years, had completely different goals and wanted to be independent. The end of that relationship I termed 'zerotime' as this was one of the hardest and loneliest times in my life. My business was a week old when I was told to leave. Today when times get tough I compare how I feel now to how I felt in 'zerotime'. I survived that time and know I can handle anything life serves me.

When applying for various jobs I was told my new masters degree was of little value. Dietitians had always been poorly paid. I decided if I was going to go broke in business it might as well be for a decent amount. Going from America to Hamilton was a real shock. Back then, Hamilton was a small town and very conservative. I knew that if I could be successful in Hamilton, I could make it anywhere.

The first business action was to interview accountants. Several accountants said to me 'it's a great idea, how long are you going to play with this before you decide to get married?' I was furious. It took me sometime to find one who would take me seriously as a woman and not think my business was a toy I was playing with until I found someone to support me for the rest of my life. Thankfully I think times are changing now in this respect. I had a similar problem at the bank. They wouldn't even consider giving me a loan because I had no collateral. Having just returned from the States, I had nothing, absolutely nothing. These struggles just made me all the more stubborn.

Professional advice has been absolutely essential in my business. If I knew back then, what I know now, I would've had a lot more confidence and grown a lot faster. Eventually I found an understanding accountant. He took my goals seriously and helped me get set up. I started writing to doctors and letting people know

I was available. I gave free talks and seminars for everybody who would listen to me. I went to Rotary, Plunket, women's groups, sports clubs, anyone that would hear me speak about what I believed in. I also started a part-time job working at the Waikato Polytechnic teaching chefs, which relieved the financial burden. Living off $90 a week, $30 for rent, $30 for petrol, and $30 for food and other expenses was really hard. I was still determined to cure the world with a lettuce leaf and a bean sprout. These days I am more realistic.

I can still remember my first paying client. I was so excited, someone actually wanted to pay me. My first appointments in those days were about an hour and a half long! I had no guidelines to go by, and absolutely no idea what worked and what didn't. I gave people far too much information, more than they could possibly absorb. It was overkill. I realised if I did such a good job on the first visit, people wouldn't come back and see me. There was no way they could remember everything! I quickly learnt there had to be follow-up appointments.

Everyone told me I was hopeless at charging people, and I was, absolutely hopeless. I had this 'hospital mentality' in the beginning, where we never charged for our services. Today with "user-pays' things have changed but back then I felt like I was stealing from people asking them to pay me. But, I forgot I wasn't being paid a salary. When I look back it's no wonder I wasn't earning a living, I wasn't charging anything! Because I had no business skills, I just divided up my hours, and thought that was what I had to charge to break even. I never thought about profit, tax, and everything else, and having a little bit left over for repairs and emergencies.

Our University and Dietetic training never covered receiving payment or the financial value of our work. I now have a very healthy attitude towards what I have earned, the effort I have put in, and what things cost me. I'm a lot more aware of what my bottom line is today. In the early days I had no bottom line, in fact I had no line! Today when people walk into my clinic, I am working for them. That's how I dealt with the financial side. I now work out my hourly rate by including all my rents, testing costs, a value on my time, factoring in taxes, GST, and then coming up with a number that I think is feasible in the market place. I could possibly charge more than I do, but I still have an ethical value to be affordable and accessible to all people as much as possible.

As I started to make a bit more headway, people started offering me money to speak at meetings and conferences, and paying my travel expenses. Things were starting to look better. I enlisted the services of a marketing manager. He is still with me today, after twelve years working together. He actually arrived as a patient at a time when I was trying to put a brochure together to explain my services. Up until then I was doing everything myself. These days I'm embarrassed about the photocopied handouts I used to put together. They were appalling!

I worked hideous hours then and I still do today. I work from 7am til 7pm most weekdays and I work most weekends. That's just the way it is. I have an unusual career. One that doesn't have a history or a clearly defined pathway. I still spend time educating people about what I do and how they would benefit from my services. I've had to work to change the whole philosophy behind using a dietitian. In the past, when people saw a dietitian it's because they were really sick and in hospital where the service is free. I've worked hard to get the doctors' support as well as medical insurers', so they realise what we're doing is helpful and preventative. There is still a long way to go and the science of nutrition is constantly changing.

I often talk about 'we'. It's actually just me, me and my computer.

But I also think about 'we' in terms of all the other dietitians who have gone through this as well, there's a couple of us that were first. This tendency to talk in plurals is because I don't ever think I have done all this by myself. There are a lot of people who have come into my life and offered knowledge or assistance in some way, from family and friends to my lawyer. You need a good support structure to do something unusual like this. It's never on your own. You might be the impetus of it all, but you succeed with the help from the support structure you create around you.

My market research came from my experiences in America. I could see people wanted unbiased professional knowledge and practical nutritional advice. It actually took a long time for New Zealanders to switch on. Today nutrition is one of the fastest growing areas. When I returned to New Zealand announcing what I was going to do, people thought I was on another planet, thinking I'd be broke within weeks. There have been several times when it's been pretty close. But I had done the market research, and I had a gut instinct that I could make it work. I figured if I believed in myself, then I'd be okay. I knew the moment I doubted myself, everyone else would too, and then it would never happen. I'm one of those people, if you tell me I'm going to fail, I dig my toes in even deeper!

"Begin...then see it completed." This has become a doctrine I live by. It is a little saying I found somewhere when I was about fourteen years old. I cut it out and have kept it ever since. The way I read the message is 'don't start anything you can not see yourself finishing'. When I started in business I had a vision in my mind. I apply this motto now when I write a book or set any goal. I can actually see how I want the finished product to look or to be. If I can't visualise something completed then I struggle to see how it can be done. Once I can see an end point I then work backwards to plan how to proceed. The trick is to keep things simple and straightforward.

Over the years nutrition has become more scientific and research based. People demand more knowledge and information today and they are more interested. My ability to communicate with patients has improved dramatically. I feel I am much am more effective today because of what I have learnt over the years. It hasn't been a smooth run, there've been many ups and downs. But I'd have to say there have been more ups than downs and every time I have been close to chucking it in and running away back to America, something happens to keep me in New Zealand. Today I am privileged to work with many different sports teams. Opportunities such as working with the America's Cup, working with the New Zealand Rugby Development Academy, New Zealand Rugby Sevens and the Kiwi league team, being re appointed to the Warriors, working with the Commonwealth Games (Auckland, 1990) and going to Brazil with the Whitbread yacht race, have all kept me here when things have been getting tough.

The first elite team I began working with was the New Zealand Rowing team. I've worked with them over the last twelve years now, depending on funding. When an athlete does well, it's very rewarding to think you are a very small piece of the puzzle that's helped that athlete get to where they are. Different sports teams take up varying amounts of time, depending on the team, the sport, and what's happening in the sporting year. I spend a great deal of time with rugby players during the off season. Before the Sydney Olympics, my time was spent finetuning athlete's diets to help them be prepared for the competition. There's been a huge amount of work involved in the America's Cup. The work involved with the BT Challenge and the Whitbread Round the World Yacht Race (now to be called the Volvo) is phenomenal. I am responsible for all the crews food and nutritional requirements. I find these extreme events so interesting, it doesn't seem like work.

My working life is quite varied, and ranges from lecturing, clinics and writing to media work. At times when nutrition issues are in the news, TV and radio stations may request a comment. Most of my work though, is one on one, helping people achieve their nutritional goals, like a nutrition coach. I analyse an individuals eating patterns, their goals, and try to match them together with nutritional recommendations they need to follow. My clients can range from people with medical issues such as heart disease, diabetes, or eating disorders; to an elite athlete; or maybe a first time marathoner, or just someone who wants more energy and to eat healthier. Much of the work I do is very personal and very private. One of the biggest rewards for me is working with children with weight problems. As you work with them, you see their personalities change dramatically. To get children, and adults, to lose weight and watch their self-confidence grow is just wonderful. I'm very practical in what I ask people to do regarding their food and exercise programmes. I make sure they have realistic and achievable goals. Debunking diet myths and getting people back to reality, is a major area of my work.

As an author I now regularly write articles for magazines. This actually started by accident. Working with John Kirwan during his early All Black days, I handed him all these handouts on sports nutrition. He replied 'Jen, this is great, but can't you put them all in a book or something'. Looking at my computer I thought, yes there probably is a book here. That was literally the impetus for my first book – Eat to Compete. I researched for eighteen months and then wrote for another eighteen months before sending the first draft off to a publisher. At that time there wasn't anything like it available. The first portion of the book concerns general nutrition for all New Zealanders while the second half focussed on sports nutrition. Up until then, I never thought I would write a book, it wasn't even a goal I had set myself.

At this time I was lecturing in the catering department at the Waikato

Polytechnic, plus running my private practice. I commuted to the four clinics around the Waikato area. I'd work all day, go for a run, have some dinner, and then begin to write from 8pm until midnight. Then I'd get up in the morning and do it all again. On the weekend I would write all Friday night through to lunchtime Saturday. On a good weekend I'd have from lunchtime Saturday until noon on Sunday off to give myself a twenty four hour break. Then I'd write from midday on Sunday until midnight. Sometimes I would get so engrossed in the topic I'd work right through the night. Twice I realised I was still tapping away at my computer at dawn and I had to be lecturing at 8.30am! I'd go for a run, have a shower, give the lecture, return home and finish the chapter I was working on, sleep a couple of hours and then get on with my day. I could do that when I was younger, but I don't think I would get away with that now. My body wouldn't cope the same. Often I was so involved in what I was doing I simply didn't notice the time.

My friends were and remain very supportive. Every so often they'd ring and say 'Jen, we haven't seen you for weeks, it's time we went out for dinner'. You need to have very understanding friends when you're working like this. Some people are offended and think they're being snobbed when you say you can't go out because you need to finish a chapter, or whatever. I couldn't have flatmates while I was writing, either, because it was too disruptive. I would wake up in the middle of the night with a good sentence floating around in my head and I'd have to get up and start writing. It would drive people crazy, computer keys going tap, tap, tap in the middle of the night.

The writing part of my career just fell into place. Reed, my publishers, have been incredibly supportive. There was a lot of editing involved in my first book. We edited 90,000 words out of Eat to Compete, and it's still a huge book. Debate was quite intense over editing decisions and there are probably a few editors out there who don't like me, but at the end of the day it's my name on the front cover and they need to understand that. Discussion between writers, editors and publishers is healthy. If you're not happy with something, you have to be honest and say so. You have to make sure you're happy with the finished product, because your reputation is at stake. My skill is in taking the technical, scientific information and translating the knowledge in a way most people can relate to personally or understand. People often tell me they can see or hear me talking when they read my books, which is a real compliment. The books are usually written the way I talk, easy to read, user-friendly, and not full of scientific jargon. I want people to be able to just pick up my books and read. I don't want nutrition to be put in the too-hard basket.

I have a bracelet with nine diamonds placed around it, one for each book I've written. There is a space for one more diamond and that book will be finished by the end of 2001. Ten books completed and another one of my goals will be completed. I also write a couple of columns for newspapers and magazines now. Initially I was terrified of writing. I can't spell to save my life, I'm slightly dyslexic, and I've got some learning disability things going on. I love my computer, it picks up my spelling mistakes and grammatical errors so I can just type away. I'd like to work on videos and teaching aids to help teachers in schools make nutrition more fun and interesting for students. Maybe I will take a diversion into an educational path for a while.

I probably stayed in Hamilton longer than I should have. The Polytechnic didn't want me to leave, but eventually I had to – I needed to grow in different areas. A number of factors combined to help me make the move to Auckland. The public hospital established and funded free clinics in the areas around the Waikato where I was operating my private clinics. I closed these clinics, sold my practice and within eighteen months I was working in Auckland fulltime.

Looking back I could have gone straight to Auckland from America, but I think it would have been harder – I learned how to manage and run my business in Hamilton and could make more mistakes there. I commuted between Auckland and Hamilton for seven years. I had two flats, and effectively lived between two cities. A group of doctors asked me to come and work with them in Auckland. I started a clinic in the city (Newmarket) and my business grew quickly. I think I've always had an Auckland personality. I love it here, I love the lifestyle, I love how busy it is. I don't even mind the traffic. (I always have work in the car!)

Clinic location is very important to my business. When I was in Hamilton I learnt very quickly that the closer you were to people, the more likely they were to come and see you. I divided Auckland into different areas, and now operate four clinics. I made the commitment to travel. It's easier for me to travel to a clinic than it is for fifty patients to travel to see me and for them to find parking. I also have flexible clinic hours, ranging between 7am and 7pm.

With the various clinics across the city and many other things going on, I've learnt very good time management skills. I get by with a great diary, and I diary everything! The usual birthdays, meetings and appointments but also housework, rest breaks, even phone calls to my friends. I have a routine at the moment where I spend Mondays writing and doing my bookwork (which I absolutely loathe). I think the government should pay me to do their GST. The remainder of the week is spent at one of the clinics. My other commitments are fitted in around the clinics. People usually book me well in advance now for public speaking engagements. I'm very proactive about keeping my articles and columns written in advance of when they are needed. If I'm going away to a conference or overseas, I'll write several articles to keep me covered during that time. If extra things come up I can usually fit them in either straight away, or in two weeks time. It's all about planning.

My day is pretty full and I am never bored. I'm up at 5.30 / 6am and start consulting at 7am. I can only consult for about six hours of one on one before I get tired. I always have other work with me wherever I am working. My at-task time is quite high, I very rarely waste any time. I am a great list writer but I don't prioritise my list. Usually I choose something easy, then something hard, and just work through it. Obviously things with deadlines get done earlier. It's that old story, if you want something done, ask a busy person. I don't muck around, I just knuckle down and get it done. I'm a great finisher – I love to cross tasks off my list, it's very rewarding.

As a soletrader I work under my own name, which has advantages and disadvantages. I have an international reputation now, especially in food for distance yacht racing events. The disadvantage is I can't sell the business on. I can sell the client base, but not the company name. My reputation is always on the line. It's my name and it's up to me to look after it. If people are disappointed, it's my fault and responsibility, no one else's.

From time to time I have had other people working for me, but I find this quite difficult. I'm probably quite a difficult person to work for. I need to learn that other people will get the job done, although they may do it differently. Because my name is going out with their work, I'm a bit more conscious of what they're doing and probably check up on them more than I should. I also think people look at my lifestyle and think working for me will be easy. They don't actually realise how hard I work! I don't believe you'll meet a single businesswoman that doesn't work horrendous hours. I really admire those women who have professional lives and run a family as well. That's got to be a nightmare, but I guess they do it because they love it. I'm lucky, I don't have any extra commitments. I can be completely focussed on my work.

When I first started my business, I was $20,000 in debt from my education in the USA and interest rates were about 28%. I'm possibly about three years behind financially because of that. Instead of worrying about money, I went without. For two and a half years I didn't go to the movies, I didn't do anything that cost money. I was totally committed to getting rid of the debt. I worked as a chef in an old people's home over the summer, to earn some cash flow to try to get on top of the debt. I poured every cent I earned into paying off this loan. I hate owing money. I'm also obsessed with taxes. I always have to know I have money to cover my taxes, sitting in the bank. It's interesting, when I had nothing to lose I took a lot more risks with the business. Today despite having a nice home and car I still have a thrifty mentality. I never buy something unless I need it. Slowly, I am learning to enjoy the benefits of my hard work, but I still sit down and work out how many times I'll wear something before I buy new clothes!

I still hate borrowing money and I'm a compulsive saver. I cried when I got my first mortgage. When I had to sign the papers I was shaking, I couldn't believe I could owe the bank that much money. Generally I'd rather not do something if it involves borrowing money. If I know I'm running out of brochures, or letterheads, I cut back on my personal drawings so I can stack up cashflow to pay for them. I wish I had more courage and faith in my accounting skills to allow myself to borrow x amount of dollars, knowing I can pay it off. But I get tense about it. I don't want to have that debt hanging over my head. This all stems from my time in the USA when the financial value of my scholarship was reduced due to changes in the rate of the New Zealand dollar. Food, rent and daily living was tough. I am not a quitter but I came really close at that time and don't ever want to be in that position again.

I think this attitude towards money has probably hindered my business growth, but I'm comfortable with where I am. I don't need to be the biggest, classiest dietitian. I want to be good at what I'm doing, well respected and have an excellent clientele. I want the respect and professionalism that goes with being one of New Zealand's top dietitians, but not necessarily the personal wealth. Having knowledge as a product is not like selling cars, or shoes, or carpet. I constantly have to convince my clients that what I'm about to tell them is worth paying for.

I don't really think of myself as a big planner or goal setter, but I do set rewards for myself. I have a weird list on my wall, which I've had for many years. There are all the crazy things I've ever wanted to do on the list and hardly any of them are work related. Number one is to go to the moon for lunch! You need to have something wacky on the list, because you never know what could happen in the future. There are other things on the list such as bungy jumping, riding in a hot air balloon, and going to an African game park. It's not a list of things I have to do, but things I'd like to do just for me. I also have a little ritual with my business goals. Every year on the 31st of December, as I transfer diaries, I write a list of ten things I'd like to achieve in my business for the New Year. Sometimes things carry over from the previous year, maybe a book has taken longer, or life has pushed things over time. In the back of my mind I have these goals for the year so there is always something to do.

The biggest disadvantage in being self-employed is lack of support when things are tough or difficult. I don't have anyone to help me when I screw up, or to share my successes if I win an award. But the advantage is I'm in charge of my own destiny. That has rewards all of its own. I know if I make a mistake I'm accountable, but I also have the freedom to experiment. I'm not controlled by a structure or an organization. Thankfully I have several friends I can discuss issues with and ask 'if this was happening to you, what would you do?' But, no matter how much support and professional advice you have, you've got to make all the decisions. If you're not a good decision maker, being self employed is not for you. If you can't hang onto something, take a bite out of it, and own it, then you're better off on a salary.

When you start a business you have to be patient, really patient. It's never going to happen as fast as you think it will. Get good people around you that can give you lots of support and never stop believing in yourself, particularly if you're doing something a bit different. If it doesn't work one time, one way, don't give up, you might have to try again from a different angle. People say life is a learning curve, well it's actually a line and it goes straight up!

Don't be afraid to make mistakes, but make sure you learn from them. Above all do not repeat them! There are downsides to success in business. Because I'm well known publicly, people comment on what I eat in restaurants. If I do something wrong I get overly criticised. People have high expectations and let you know they're disappointed if you don't live up to them. Some people have called me a workaholic, a term I really hate. They try to justify my chosen lifestyle, based on their terms. I love my work and my work is a big part of who I am, but I'm not a workaholic. I can and do take time off, but people often only see me from a business point of view. I like to keep my private life and relationships very private.

My advice to others is to get as much information about running a business as you can. I hate accounting, I'm not a number person at all. I know that's my weakness and I wish I had more skills in that area. Luckily I have an accountant who encourages me to get things done. Another important thing in starting a business is to get your timing right. I'm sure I was fortunate I started this career in the very early stages. People have seen me make a career out of nutrition, but they can't be me, they have to do it differently and find their own way.

I love what I do. You need to have that passion to make it happen and to believe in your self. " Begin…then see it completed."

Amanda Dunlop

Amanda Dunlop

HCH FORMULAS LTD

Amanda was a single mother with a three year old son when she decided to take on a five year course studying classical homeopathy. Now, as well as running her own homeopathic clinic, her involvement with endurance and multi-sport racing has led to her developing her own product range of homeopathic formulas.

I had been living in Queenstown for nine years, with a pretty varied work history, before I decided to move to Christchurch and study classical homeopathy. I was the first female qualified raft guide in NZ, I'd had an interior design business for three years, I'd been a 4WD tour guide, and I'd worked on the sales team for one of the local resorts.

Ben was three when I decided to move to Christchurch. I did two part-time years and three fulltime years, it was really hard work. I was studying, bringing up a child on my own, and managing a restaurant at night to pay the bills.

When I finished my course I decided to return to Queenstown, which was quite a hard decision, having lived there for nine years and then left. But I'd started practicing part-time at the Natural Health Centre, in Queenstown. I used to come and go, once a month, and because I already had a client base, I thought I might as well move back. That was good. It meant I had a bigger practice than my contemporaries in Christchurch, where there were more homeopaths practicing.

I was pretty exhausted after five years of studying. I was on holiday when a friend told me he had some information about a new 500km team multi-sport race, in the States, called the Eco Challenge. I had done support for him on the Coast to Coast race with my homeopathic medicines. I asked him if he needed a support crew for The Eco Challenge and he said 'yeah, we do'. So I told him to put me down for it, it sounded great. For me that meant moving heaven and earth really, packing Ben up to his Dad, then packing up and renting out my house. But I did it and I went to the States for three months and did the support work for this team in the first Eco Challenge. The team did so well in the race, they were asked to go to another race in Maine ten weeks later. I did support for that race as well. In between races I spent four weeks at a homeopathic college in San Francisco attending classes and observing practitioners. I was seeing a pattern developing in the different remedies I was giving the athletes for the conditions they were finding themselves in physically, mentally, and emotionally, and started developing formulations to deal with their symptoms.

Because I was classically trained, I was used to giving single remedies, formulations were not regarded as the way to go. But in France, there's a homeopathic pharmacy on every corner, where they mostly prescribe combination remedies. I started thinking about the problems I was seeing at the races, and looking at how different remedies could work in together.

An American team I met at the Eco Challenge, decided to come out and do the Southern Traverse, a similar adventure race based in New Zealand. I did the support work for them and they loved the homeopathic medicine. One of the guys said to me, 'you should be doing these formulas under your own label, you should produce this brand yourself'. It had never occurred to me to do the formulations under my own brand. I was getting the homeopathic pharmacy to make up the formulas in the traditional tablet form, under their label.

The tablets weren't ideal. You had to fiddle around popping lids, trying to get only one tablet out and then put it under your tongue and let it dissolve. When athletes have been racing for six days, they've barely got any saliva left so the last thing they want to be doing is sucking on a dry tablet. But, they did work. The athletes were telling me they liked the formulas.

So I borrowed a friend's computer, sat down in my office and worked out a business plan. That took me about two months. I really thought hard about how I could take a traditional medicine and make it useable for athletes who are out running or cycling. Basically I came up with lightweight, plastic, pump spray bottles, with formulations made up in liquid form. Since then it's been a four year trial and development process.

It took six months to get the formulations right and develop the packaging. When I was looking for packaging I felt really cut off, not being in one of the major centres. For the first eighteen months

I was supporting Telecom. Then it was a matter of developing a branding awareness, designing a logo, choosing colours, getting a brochure together.

There have been hurdles at every stage. The first lot of labels I had were a complete disaster. I gave every team in the 1996 Southern Traverse a bottle of Endurance – one of the formulas. That was the first time anyone saw the formulas in the new spray bottle form. But, all the labels fell off as soon as they got wet, so they were all left with blank bottles, not knowing what was in them. I'm on the third generation of labels now and I've finally got that one sussed.

The next process was getting friends of mine, local athletes, to trial the products and give me feedback. They were very supportive of the fact I was developing this 'weird' sort of medicine, that was completely drug free, and was going to help them do what they wanted to do. So they were very helpful with their comments, feedback and general support.

Everything has taken a long time, but I have really tried to do everything well. Each phase has been relatively expensive to develop but I think it will be worthwhile in the long run.

The Otago Business Development Board was really supportive. They thought the concept was strange, and they didn't really understand it, but they were positive about it and gave me a couple of grants including one to explore overseas markets. I was lucky, I got in just before they canned it.

Everyone I talked to thought it was a great, innovative idea. The hardest part was educating people to accept the product and try it. I've found the best way is to go to races and represent the product myself. The first year I got permission to promote my products at the Coast to Coast. I rocked up there with my little HCH Formulas vest on, and spent two and a half days just talking to athletes and giving out brochures. That was the first time Canterbury, and that field of athletes, had seen the product and they were really interested in it. But, they need to see it, and see it again, and then maybe they'll try it, and once you can get them to try it, they really like it.

It's been a slow process getting people familiar with the product, but I've been going to as many races as I can. I go to the Ironman, the Southern Traverse, Coast to Coast, as well as the Eco Challenge and many other international races. People are getting used to seeing me, seeing the banner and the products. The New Zealand athletes know about the products now, and the overseas athletes are interested because the Kiwi's are using them.

The latest phase is marketing and distribution, which I think is the hardest part so far. I'm sure many people have a great product, but it disappears because they don't have the right marketing, or enough capital to keep the marketing going. There seems to be a critical point where you hear "I was given your product to try and I liked it, but I don't know where to get it" more and more often. I have been very selective about how I want to distribute the product. I made the choice not to pack up the car boot and travel around to every appropriate retail store, selling it. I know that I don't have time to be on the road, I also don't have the finance to hold their credit. I would rather take a cut in margin and have two or three key distributors carrying that debt.

This has been a very slow way to go, finding the right people, catching the attention of someone who will look at the product and think 'this looks interesting'. I feel I've chosen the slow road, but it seems to be what I can deal with. Every now and again I think ' oh no, it's been four years and I haven't made my first million yet'.

Then I think, 'hang on, it doesn't matter if it takes ten years, as long as you can still eat in the meantime!'

Every year it gets stronger and stronger. This year, I've made a lot of progress with distribution. The products are available in the US through an internet website. I have a distributor in the UK who's a veteran gold medal cyclist. I am currently doing a test of fifty pharmacies in Brisbane to launch the products in Australia. I have a New Zealand distributor specialising in cycling outlets. And I've just signed a distribution deal with Naturopharm, one of the leading homeopathic pharmacies in New Zealand, which will see the products in about ninety percent of pharmacies and healthfood stores nationwide.

I've found you have to be very careful in dealing with potential distributors. I'm not in a position where I can take a big risk. I had a distribution agreement signed up with a guy in Australia. He gave me my first order and it was incredibly exciting to have such a big, off-shore order. But then when it came to adhering to the schedule of payment, he starting sending me email messages with all sorts of excuses, and I thought 'oh, no'. The initial stock still hasn't been paid for! This was a hard lesson, but because I was cautious about the initial amount of stock sent, the loss hasn't wiped out the business.

It's quite easy to fall into these traps when you get excited and put your faith in people. I spent a year dealing with an American company. I did an exploratory trip to the US and went to a big Natural Product Expo there. Like a lot of American companies, this company promised me the Earth, they thought the product was wonderful. All of a sudden, bang, they'd picked up on something else. For me it was some German corporation with another new product line.

The latest hurdle in distribution has come via the Health Department. Drug companies have been steadily losing business over the last few years because of an increased awareness in natural products. They have lobbied the government to tighten up on natural product regulations. To protect the consumer you can't claim natural products are capable of curing anything. It's not actually legal to present any information to consumers about what your product can and can't do, or even give any indications for use. So before I can go ahead with my new distribution agreement I have to redevelop the brochures and change some of the labelling. The whole development process has been a continuation of hurdles. As soon as you climb one hurdle, there's another one in front of you, you just have to keep going.

When I was living in Christchurch, I bought an old house and did it up while I was studying. I used the money from selling that house as capital to get HCH Formulas off the ground. Once I'd put as much capital as I could afford into it, then it became difficult. I think if you are under capitalized, you have to be very careful about where you spend your money. I have magazines ringing me all the time wanting me to advertise. Somehow they find you out and they want you to spend $500 on an ad in a glossy magazine. That's fine if you've got the distribution and the product is out there to buy, but I haven't let myself spend money on promotion at this point, because I think it would be wasted.

Although I've had a lot of support from friends and family, I do find working in isolation very hard sometimes. Every now and then I come to a grinding halt. When you're working by yourself, there's no one there to talk things through, and bounce ideas off. Sometimes I struggle with confidence and getting back to people. You have to be persistent and keep persevering. I find that I will roll on with the project for about eighteen months, full steam ahead, and then 'crash', my motivation and confidence just seems to go 'puff'. You get into a slump and start getting paranoid that it's not going to work. Usually something positive comes along, you muster up your energy, and get the ball rolling again. I find the best thing to do when I feel like that is to make myself go and talk to someone. I think maintaining contact with people at that time is really valuable. Often just by talking through the issues you can see something that you can cope with doing. If you can pick up any little thing and get something achieved, that's often enough to get the ball rolling again.

Professional advice from lawyers and accountants was very important in setting up my business. Although I found it quite difficult to get practical, down to earth help. My first accountant was a real good talker, but I'd come out of his office thinking 'what am I actually walking away with that I can practically use?' And, my bank manager was really good, before the bank system changed. I was used to being able to pop in and talk to my local bank manager and then one day I was told I couldn't see him directly anymore, I had to ring a number. I hate dealing with those big, impersonal banking systems.

Another person who was really useful in the early days was a business consultant. I had been working away on the project and then I got to a brick wall, I was completely stuck. It was an expensive exercise but I went to see this woman and she sat me down in her office and pulled all the stuff out of my head. We put all this stuff from my head up around the walls, and then she condensed it into sheets of what needed to be done and when, and formulated all these systems for me. I came away with something manageable. Instead of having this huge conglomeration of information racing around in my head, I had pages telling me that this week I had to do this and this, and by the end of the month I had to have that done. This really helped me focus on what was important and gave me a clearer sense of direction.

I tend to work frantically, with sixteen things on the go at any one time. I find it really helpful to sit down and write a timeline. I have to list things I want to achieve by the end of the day, the end of the week, the end of the month. When you're feeling overwhelmed, and there're a million things floating around in your head, it really helps to get it all down on paper and then it's not nearly so daunting.

I keep HCH Formulas completely separate to the homeopathic clinic, so although they complement each other, they are two different businesses. The clinic is part time, about two and a half days a week, and the rest of the time I'm working on my product range. Doing both works well for me. As a classical homeopath, treating patients, I get a lot of fulfilment but there's only a certain amount of energy I can put into it. Developing this commercial range of products has allowed my capitalist side to come into play.

I've recently had to rethink my workspace. Because I was away a lot with the product range, my patient load at the clinic decreased significantly. My accountant pointed out I couldn't afford to keep my office in town that I was only using a quarter of the time. This was quite a hard change for me to make as I always felt working from home wouldn't work for me. My son is away at boarding school and I live alone now, so I was reluctant to have my office there as well. It's important to me to be in town, maintaining contact with people. But eventually reality had to strike, I just couldn't afford to keep my office.

Now I have a consultation room in town, which I share with a group of practitioners. That's cut down my overheads by a huge amount. And, I have a home office where I do all my HCH Formulas work. I have changed the way I work quite considerably and I think I work much more efficiently by keeping the two businesses in separate locations. Before I would be constantly switching hats, now I am much more focussed when I'm in either workspace. It's also much better for my patients. When I'm in my consultation room, I am one hundred percent focussed on the classical homeopathic practice, there're no phones ringing or faxes coming through with HCH business.

I've found working from home much better than I thought it would be. I'm glad I kept a consultation room in town, though. I have also got together with another woman who's set up a business that is quite complementary to mine. We get together once a week and exchange contacts and ideas, and if we have any problems we can talk about them. I think that's really important.

I find women do business in a much more supportive manner than men, they're not driven by the same 'someone has to lose' mentality. It's been interesting, in running my own business, dealing with some of the men out there. You have to front up in quite a strong way for them to take you seriously. Some men have been quite chauvinistic in their approach to me, so I tend to be quite clear in my communications of what I think and then they can take it or leave it.

Juggling business and bringing up a child has been quite hard. The early years when I was studying, working, and bringing up Ben were actually really hard. My family were very supportive. But I did stretch myself to the limit. At the end of those five years I was absolutely exhausted. I'm lucky that Ben is a great kid. He's been very patient and understands when I have to work. Also, women can do ten things at once, whereas men tend to be more one dimensional. He's at boarding school now and he loves it. It's actually quite hard for me not having him around, I miss him. The times that I'm with him now are wonderful, I give up work when he's here. The time is precious, so we make the effort to go off on adventures and make the most of the quality time together.

When I started the homeopathic course in 1990, I had an idea of homeopathic medicine, but I didn't understand the full depth of it. If I had known how difficult the five years would be, I don't know whether I would have done it. The development of my own product range has also been a huge undertaking, it's much bigger than I ever dreamt it would be at the beginning. You just have to keep persisting and persevere each time you hit a hurdle. I have been over and around so many brick walls. When one door shuts, you just have to keep going until another one opens. The personal satisfaction of creating a product that benefits people in their everyday lives is tremendous. Despite the ongoing challenges, I wouldn't have it any other way.

Sarah Brown

Sarah Brown

FOOLPROOF

Sarah Brown was working for the Ministry of Forestry in Wellington and at a point in her career where the only way up was to apply for a managerial position and leave behind the hands-on work she loved. She opted out of the government department to set up her own business - Foolproof - specialising in proofreading and editing. Not wanting to be perceived as a "freelancer", Sarah has always focussed on building a reputation as a professional business.

I started Foolproof back in 1995. Previously I'd completed a degree in English and worked for about twelve years both in New Zealand and overseas, doing a variety of jobs. I worked for the BBC for a while – directing transmission for BBC1 and BBC2. Then I spent a couple of years doing sales and marketing for a graphic design company and discovered I wasn't particularly good at cold-calling so probably sales and marketing wasn't really for me! That job was good for networking, though, with the result that one of my clients, the Ministry of Forestry, invited me to apply for a job with them in communications. I had no idea what communications involved but they seemed to think I'd be good at it. My application was successful and I worked for them for three years. It was while working there I discovered that I was good at managing publications, editing and proofreading.

After three years my manager resigned and I was ready for a change. It was decision time for me: did I apply for the manager position, or did I move into another organization and basically do the same thing somewhere else? I decided I didn't want to do either. I didn't see myself as a manager, which was a tough decision as some of my colleagues were encouraging me to apply. But I like doing the hands-on stuff, seeing projects through. I don't like going to lots of meetings and all the political side of it.

I decided that I would go out alone and set up my own business. Having been in the situation of looking for proofreaders and finding them very difficult to find, especially good ones, I felt there was an opening in the market there. I knew I could do editing as well so I set up with those two specialist areas – proofreading and editing.

I did agonise over the decision to set up Foolproof for quite a while. I guess I started off thinking 'someone should set up a business doing this', which progressed to 'maybe I should', and then to 'maybe I will'. I knew there was a market out there for the business through my own experience, and I knew I was good at it. I also talked to a lot of people and the response was encouraging. I decided to do it but I think I honestly expected it to fail. I don't think I ever saw it lasting beyond six months!

When I set up I really wanted people to perceive me as a business rather than a freelancer. I wanted to have an office, a brochure and everything I needed to ensure I looked professional. I found that people I'd worked with in the past were good at their job but they didn't go the extra mile to make you feel good about using their services. So I had a brochure designed by Origin and went out and let companies know I was in business. I spent two months marketing. I approached companies and the response was usually 'Oh thank goodness, we didn't know where to find someone like you'. That cold calling went down really well. Just turning up, looking professional, and having found out a bit about the organization before I got there. And the brochure was a huge hit. It was quite a different design – funky colours and minimal text. I know people have passed it on to others, so it's been a great marketing tool. Since then I haven't done any extra advertising. All my business comes from referrals and word of mouth. I've been working fulltime from the very beginning. The business just took off!

When I left the Ministry of Forestry I was quite lucky in that they contracted me back for 20 hours a week for six months. That gave me a steady income and allowed me the rest of the week to get Foolproof set up and to go out and approach potential clients. I set up in November, which was a bad time of the year, but I just took it quietly and having some money coming in really helped.

It was quite a cheap business to set up. I borrowed $15,000 from the bank, which I decided was enough for me to live on for a couple of months plus buy a computer, a printer, a cell phone, all I really needed in the office and to cover the rent. I didn't have any problems getting a bank loan. I was still in a relationship at the time, so we both went along. I had done a business plan, which they appreciated and I think the fact I had the contract with the Ministry of Forestry and a partner available to support me probably helped. Generally I've found the bank pretty helpful.

The bank was giving out materials at the time on setting up businesses and how to do a business plan. I found this a really good exercise as it made me think about some important questions like 'What am I?' 'What is my business?' 'Who will my customers be?' 'What makes my business different?' I had to work out why the bank should be interested in financing me. It clarified what I was all about, what income I was prepared to live on and what income I wanted to earn. It made me realise that I am financially quite ambitious, that I wanted to earn good money reasonably quickly. It was a really good process to go through and from that I formulated my business plan.

The business is a lot more successful than I ever imagined it would be. And it has evolved to a certain extent. I do a lot of writing now, which I never intended to do. One day a client asked me if I'd like to do some writing for them. My immediate reaction was to say ' No, I don't write'. But it was in the early stages and I didn't want to lose the business. I was always thinking this could be my last job, so I said 'yes'. I am still a bit scared of writing but it has become easily 50-60% of the business. We do all sorts – direct marketing letters, brochures, reports, articles, websites. It's very much writing with a business focus. Generally not technical, but simple, informative writing that gets a clear message across.

Occasionally clients approach us wanting more PR type work, they want a strategy. Personally, I'm not comfortable with doing that. It scares me for a start. But also I don't see it as being good for my business. We are a specialist business and I don't want to detract from that. Sometimes I allow the business to go off in a different direction, mainly depending on the client and the relationship we have with them. For some of our clients we do research projects and speech writing and the odd job that's outside our main focus but generally we are writers, editors and proofreaders – that is what we do.

I really enjoyed working by myself. I like the freedom and I find I'm a good worker on my own. I like being in control and I'm not a very good delegator. There came a point, though, when I realised I needed to employ a second person. I was working too hard and I was tired. I realised that wasn't healthy, that I didn't have a life, and that I had to do something about it. I was also having to turn away work. I'd probably wanted to do it for a while but I hadn't found the right person. Working in such a small office, that was really important. I met a woman, Kathryn, who I felt really comfortable with. I asked her if she'd be interested, and she was. It was also a question of confidence in the business that there would be enough work for two people. I have an arrangement with her where I contract her on an hourly rate. This way I don't have the overheads of being an employer, I don't have to worry about ACC and PAYE and don't have to maintain the costs of her wages.

There's only really been one downtime in the business, which lasted for three weeks. There was enough work for one but not for two. It was quite stressful. I was more worried for Kathryn, than for me. Having got through that time I think I know now the work is going to keep coming in. I have to remind myself that nobody hates me, there's no reason for the lack of work, so take the time out and make the most of the opportunity to have a break. So I did, I took days off, I started having real weekends, and when I look back at that time, on the whole it wasn't a bad month.

I sometimes miss working on my own. But I also realise that because I charge by the hour, if it's just me then I'd have to work a lot of hours to earn good money. That's a crazy way to live. If I want to maintain my lifestyle, have more time off, and get further reward from my business, then the only way to do that is to employ more people. I have to admit that's the only reason I'm considering expanding and employing extra staff, otherwise I'd rather it was just me.

For a business like Foolproof, location is quite important in terms of logistics. People know I'm in the city, so in terms of getting to clients, it's really handy. Most of the work I do is incredibly tightly turned around. Clients phone and say 'can you come around now', it's no problem, I'll be there in five minutes. Generally clients don't come to me so they don't see how small our office is! Ideally I'd like to get into a situation where I could share office space with other complementary businesses. Each business could share services and resources, you could help each other out. For me, working from home has never appealed. I like getting up in the morning and going to work. I also feel more professional working out of an office.

Professional advice hasn't been a big part of my business. My ex-partner was in business so he helped me set up the books and he gave me a lot of helpful advice to get started. I got an accountant as soon as I set the business up. I like to do the GST and the monthly accounts so I know what's happening in the business and they take care of everything else. I always send a chocolate bar with every invoice, which seems to work well, clients love it.

There has only been one situation where I made a mistake that ended up costing me money. It was a print job and there was something I should've picked up and I didn't. I'm very paranoid about quality control. I'm also pedantic about keeping records and getting things in writing. I find it's really important to go back at the end of a conversation and say ' I understand from this, that this is what you want' and agreeing and writing it down. I always put a full disclaimer on my work so my responsibility finishes once my job is done.

I don't really do any advertising but I send out fun things to clients every now and then just to keep in touch. I did that a lot when I first set up, which helped to get my name circulating. When I moved offices I got some pencils done with Foolproof on them and attached them to the change of address card. After six months I sent out tags with erasers attached just saying 'keep in touch'. One winter I sent my clients vitamin C tablets saying I hope their winter is 'flooproof'. I find that's been a really good way of keeping in touch with clients. I usually send out Christmas gifts too. One year I had dictionaries done with Foolproof covers, another year I did a Foolproof bookmark. It's just a little extra and it's my way of saying thank you to clients for their business.

Support is vital in business. Initially outside support gave me the belief that I could do it. Support from my friends has always been a given and my clients have been great but business-wise I am largely on my own. I would love a mentor and I've been looking for one. I also read in a business magazine an article about a life coach, which I quite like the idea of.

I went to a seminar recently where they said that every week you should take at least 24 hours off where there is absolutely no work done whatsoever. That's quite hard when you're running your own business. There seems to always be things to do and because you want your business to succeed, you want to work all the time. I started making myself take 24 hours a week off and I'm finding it's working really well. I've discovered if I plan to do things for myself, somehow the work stops to allow me to do it. Planning is very important in terms of the day to day running of my business. I make lists and tick everything off as I go. Long term planning is on my list of things to do, but unfortunately has been a low priority. I think it's time to sit down and do another business plan and work out where Foolproof is going. It's very easy when the business is going well to just sit back and think 'oh well, I'll just carry on'. I think I really need to look at what kind of work is coming in, maybe if it came in this year, it will come again next year, and we can be more proactive in getting that repeat business instead of just waiting for it to come to us. If I'm serious about expanding then I need to develop the business plan and shape what is going to happen next. If I want to employ an extra person, we need more work, which will require more marketing. Another option is to take a bigger risk and set up in a different country. I know now the business works.

The hardest thing I find about being in business is turning jobs down. And not being able to take a holiday, because you're scared you'll lose clients and you're scared of not earning any money for that time. There is a paranoia that one day it will all dry up and nobody will like you anymore. I find it very hard to say no to work. Usually I say yes unless it really is totally impossible. Then I will work nights and weekends to get the job done.

I enjoy being a woman in business. I like the way women operate and I like dealing with men in business. I think the key is to be confident, take the risk. To me any decision is a risk, there's no such thing as a serious risk unless you're talking millions of dollars. Risks are challenges, opportunities. And if it goes wrong you can always go back to the beginning. I always thought if Foolproof doesn't work I can just go back to working for someone else again. What have you got to lose?

Louise
Rutten

Louise Rutten

INKSPOT DIGITAL LTD

Louise is the driving force behind Inkspot Digital Ltd– an Auckland based IT / Animation / Entertainment company leading the world in computer animation. This small youthful company works alongside big players such as Microsoft and shows the world what a couple of Kiwis can achieve when they put their minds to it. For Louise, the secrets to success don't lie behind a university degree or loads of investment capital – success comes from lots of hard work, personality, and an undying belief in your idea.

Inkspot Digital started out as three people – myself with a real passion for sales and marketing and two animators, both also very passionate. That passion continues to be the bottom line for our company. I actually met Mark and Paul (the other two founding directors) while I was employed as the Sales and Marketing Manager for an American sportswear and apparel company. I hired them to do some work for me on a contract we had with the Super 12. I really admired their work and Mark and I worked extremely well together. They were solely a production company. What they were lacking was any form of sales and marketing expertise. I can remember being in the car park one day and Mark said "I'd really like to employ you". I laughed and replied " you'd never be able to afford me, not in a million years!' He was sure he'd be able to work it out somehow. As it turned out I got made redundant. I didn't want to go back to the corporate world so I decided to set up my own company – Exclaim! We also started a company together – Inkspot Digital –and just for the record, he still can't afford me!

My background is publishing and advertising. I set up Exclaim! as an advertising and marketing contract company. We held contracts with Conde Naste for all the Vogue titles and with other New Zealand publishers. I ran that company for three years, which paid me to be able to work on Inkspot Digital at the same time. I can honestly say we all worked truly horrendous hours for a long time when we started Inkspot Digital. Twenty hours a day, seven days a week was quite normal. It's only recently we've stopped working such huge hours and we still do 16 – 18 hour days. Even now I'm eight months pregnant I still work 12-14 hour days! Yes it's tiring, but it's great – we're doing what we love. We are all 100% committed to making Inkspot Digital work and the only way to fund that for a long time was for all of us to have other sources of income.

My passion and love had always been for magazines. I'd worked in the industry for a long time so I had a lot of contacts, and having titles like Vogue was no great hardship! I managed to do Exclaim! on my own for about a year, alongside Inkspot Digital. As Inkspot started taking up more time and the travel was getting more extensive, I employed Giscard (Gis), my husband, to take over the marketing contracts. Eventually, Inkspot Digital was at a stage where it was starting to fly. You can only do those hours for so long so I employed salespeople to sell the advertising for Exclaim! I loved that company, I absolutely adored it. It was an extremely hard decision to sell it, but I did, quite recently.

With Inkspot Digital we saw an opportunity in the market for a clipart product for people like myself who can't draw at all. In fact, all our sales and marketing tools use my appalling stick figure drawings as an example – "if you draw like this, then you need this product!"

We wanted to produce something different, and to that end all our products have our personality stamped on them. They are very cartoony type characters and you will either love them or hate them. We are not ashamed of that - we were never trying to appeal to the entire audience. We were confident a percentage of the market would take it and think "Wow, that's really cool".

There were a lot of differentiating factors between our product and everything else that was on the market. We researched it and decided there was a gap we could fill. Most people do market analysis to find their biggest competitors and then try to figure out how they can compete with them. We took a different approach and looked at who the biggest players were in the marketplace and thought "OK, we want to play with them." You can't compete with someone like Microsoft. So we went and saw Microsoft with the aim of working alongside them and they were fantastic. We launched our first product in association with Publisher 98.

Ever since that first deal, our business has always been based on finding out who are the biggest players in the market, then working alongside them and using our products to enhance what they are doing. This is how we've been able to advance and grow in the IT industry. In the US we work with the biggest IT companies, which is definitely a strong suit.

We started with Cliptoonz Volume 1. 'Clip' for clipart, 'toon' for cartoon style and 'nz' for New Zealand. We did that with Microsoft here in New Zealand. It's been a constant good seller, which led to Volume 2. Later we brought out Clip Art for Kiwis because we found schools liked our work but they didn't have any true Kiwi images. Last year we became the first company in the world that could do micro payments on our website, so you could buy an image for a dollar. The backend technology for our website is huge! Most companies would spend years and years developing what we have developed. We are a very small team, but we've got good people, we've invested heavily in them and we have been able to develop a lot of our technology ourselves. Because of this we have managed to always be at the leading edge of what we do.

After our Cliptoonz range we developed a product called E-Toonz, which has advertising enabled content. Basically this means taking the fundamentals of a cartoon strip, animating it, putting it on the web and allowing an opportunity for it to carry advertising within it. From E-toonz we have developed a suite of products all based around animated content, communicating effectively with the target market.

The beauty of our animated cartoons is that we have traditional animators who work in Flash, as opposed to Flash programmers. Other companies generally don't have the ability to do this. Flash programmers come from a mathematical perspective whereas traditional animators understand the fundamentals of movement, acting and timing. From this base (eight years of training) traditional animators can then learn Flash programming, giving them the ability to create highly interactive characters, while still keeping file sizes small – something a Flash programmer is usually unable to achieve to such a high level.

There's a company in LA that buys this skill base from us on a per minute basis, runs them on the web, and then if they think it will sell they take it for the television networks. Companies like this one burn about two million US dollars a month just to keep the company running. There's no way that would ever happen in New Zealand – we could never sustain that sort of expenditure. These e-toonz per se, are not our core business but we continue to do them because it keeps us in with all the key people in the entertainment industry and is a base for our other products. It's a weird industry, but we play with them because they are the biggest players in the market. They see our work, which is 100 times better than what is coming out of the States and they acknowledge that. We have the edge because we are traditional animators, we maximise Flash and our files are quick and easy to download.

At Inkspot Digital we invest heavily in our people. To be a traditional animator, and to be good at it, takes at least ten years. We have people who have started with us at the age of fifteen and they've stayed with us. A big part of our company philosophy is 'dedication to our people'. We give them all the training and the opportunities to be creative that we can. We wouldn't have a company if it wasn't for the passion of the people within it. We haven't always made money, there have been a lot of sacrifices along the way, and they've all been a part of that. At the end of the day, everyone benefits when the sacrifices pay off.

We are a very youthful company - I was 26 years old when we started. The oldest person in the whole company now is the CEO who's 32 years old. I fully believe that age has nothing to do with it. It's all about attitude – particularly in the IT industry where everything is constantly changing.

Another advantage in us all being so young is that we were able to learn and make mistakes and nobody judged each other. We've always allowed ourselves to make mistakes and sometimes that's cost us money but we've never blamed each other if something goes wrong. I think most people are their own hardest taskmasters anyway, you can't say anything to someone who's made a mistake that they haven't already thought to themselves but ten times worse.

We have fifteen people at Inkspot Digital at the moment and are currently in the process of opening an office in the United States. With our 'fantastic' exchange rate at the moment, this is a very expensive exercise! Eventually we will have the Sales and Marketing office based in California and keep the creative side based in New Zealand. Keeping the creative side New Zealand based allows us to remain cost effective. Also, the people we already have in the business are so valuable to us we wouldn't want to risk losing them through re-location. The investment we have made in our team is huge, they are very important to us.

In IT, the whole industry is moving and changing on a daily basis. People talk about the importance of business plans – in the IT industry it's amazing if you can even stick to a six month business plan. New things come up and you have to jump on them, introduce the new concept and incorporate it into your ideas. It's quite hard to plan in this industry, you always have to be flexible enough to veer off suddenly on an alternative route, and yet still stay focussed and clear on the final destination.

The main key to being successful in business, I think, is you have to have so much belief in yourself, you can't take on board other people's insecurities. There will always be people out there who will think "that's a bit different, a bit risky, too difficult, too expensive". That's where a lot of people with good ideas fall over. Their great ideas never get to market because they don't fully believe in themselves, or they're not prepared to take the risk. People are always complaining there isn't enough capital in New Zealand to get ideas off the ground, and I agree with that to an extent but it's also a case of natural attrition. It is hard work, you will have to work long hours, there will be setbacks – are you cut out for it? You need an absolute undying belief in yourself right from the start to be able to last the distance.

After about eighteen months of us all working two jobs we decided that to make Inkspot Digital work we needed some real money behind us. We all mortgaged everything we had, and borrowed money from the bank. We still had to work huge hours though, because we couldn't afford to employ other people. Last year we paid off the bank loan so the company has no debt, which is a great feeling.

Recently we decided to get a private investor involved in Inkspot so we could expand. We decided that getting a bank loan wasn't beneficial to the company. Although a bank loan helps you get up and running, it doesn't bring anything extra to the table. We decided to look for an investor who would bring in contacts as well as money, and ultimately help the direction of the company through their own experience in business. That was what we were looking for, but easier said than done. We didn't know anybody like that! At that stage, there was a huge influx of dot com companies being thrown crazy amounts of cash. We were there in the American market so we saw it all the time and thought "God, it can't be that hard to get some money!" But, the reality was quite different.

We looked at New Zealand companies who portrayed themselves as IT investment companies. Unfortunately the reality was that they were old fashioned institutional investors who thought they needed to be involved in IT, but weren't able to change the way they operated to accommodate IT business. For example, they needed a minimum five year business plan. In IT, five year business plans don't exist. Of course we can speculate, but most of the technology we'll be using in two years' time hasn't been invented yet, so who knows what will be happening in five years! Eventually we employed a company who match investors with companies.

The whole investment scene was a big learning curve for us. We gave criteria for what we were looking for in an investor – basically that they would invest a portion of money into the company for a percentage of the business; they would give us the freedom and the flexibility to keep the attitude of the company the same as it had always been; yes they would give us a direction, but there was no day to day involvement; and that they understood that the passion of the company had driven it to where it was and that passion wouldn't be an issue for them. This was quite hard to find – we were basically asking somebody to hand over their money for us to spend as we saw fit! We also decided we wanted it by a certain date. We are a very driven company in terms of timeframes. We gave the company a deadline of five weeks to find us our investor, which almost gave them a heart attack. Normally just due diligence takes that long, let alone actually meeting anyone. But they were marvellous, they took on the challenge.

A number of investors looked at us and we looked at them. We narrowed it down to three possibilities. One of those was a large, privately owned investment company. We don't even measure on the Richter scale of their portfolio. They recognised the passion we had in our company and that we were very much at the leading edge of everything we were doing. They put an offer in to us and we accepted.

We've been very fortunate with them – they have been the perfect investor for us. They've got lots of contacts and they let us get on and do what we need to do. They have their CEO sit on our board and as we continue to grow, we'd hate for them not to be a part of that. They understand the importance of our creative side, but they make us focus on the dollars, and they give us different ways of looking at things. We turned down other investors to choose this company and it really was quite a scary decision. We've worked so hard to build this company and here we were selling part of it! It is quite difficult to raise funds in New Zealand. Well, perhaps not if you are prepared to give up a large chunk of your company for a small amount of money, but if you are looking for a "partner" who doesn't have to have a controlling interest and is realistic about the price of their investment, then that is hard to find. In fact, getting investment is probably the most difficult thing about being in business in this country.

One thing I don't recommend, which I'm sure goes against the grain for a lot of people, is having a mentor. A lot of people seem to have it in their head that they need one. We've never had a mentor, as such. We're all individually very strong people so we tend to think " OK, this is what we want to do, so let's go do it!" We looked at a mentoring scheme once but I found it very disappointing – I felt they set limitations on you and what you could achieve. It scares me to think people with mentors may be being held back or using it as a support mechanism. Personally I feel very dubious about mentors, I think people hang too much on them and I'm always scared that other people will suck the life and energy out of an idea. Building a business is based on gut instinct and an absolute passion for an idea, plus market knowledge. A mentor doesn't have that like you do. Having said that, I think the term "mentor" is overused and abused. We do now have somebody we respect enormously who sits on our board and gives us suggestions and ideas. I guess in the purest sense of the word he is a mentor, but this has come out of working together and building respect, not through a scheme.

You will always have doubts and there's nothing wrong with that. You have to analyse what you're doing to a degree and make sure you're doing it for the right reasons. In our first few years we never asked anybody else's opinion, we just did what we felt was right and we really went for it. Some people gave us their opinion anyway and we took it on board to a certain extent, but we always thought that if we didn't do it maybe somebody else would and we'd wish we had. Even if something doesn't work, it will always lead to other things, and you never know until you try! For us we were always prepared to take a risk. It was always a calculated risk, but still a risk nonetheless, and probably more of a risk than most people would be prepared to take.

I wouldn't change anything that we've done, even the mistakes we made, the hardships, the long hours, being tired, not making the money we thought we'd be making, and all the things that are out of your control. We have learnt so much through this business and the personal growth has been huge.

I don't know that I'm particularly inspirational as an individual, but as a company I think we definitely are, and that company comes down to individuals at the end of the day. Not one person at Inkspot Digital could ever take sole credit. We started with three directors – two animators and myself. One of the original directors has since left leaving just the two of us. Our CEO has been with us for the last couple of years, who just by coincidence also happens to be my husband. We did employ him because of his skills! He's got good strong sales & marketing skills, he's passionate about animation (he can't draw either) and he's also got a technical background so he's able to pull us all together quite nicely. He's very much a visionary, looking further down the track while we tend to work in the here and now. We all complement each other quite well. If you took away any one of us we wouldn't be. We've certainly had some struggles and financially we've all had to put everything on the line, but if you're going to do something it's got to be worth doing so throw yourself into it wholeheartedly!

There are not many women in the IT industry that I know personally and that have started their own IT companies. It's a tough industry but I don't think there're any particular barriers for women especially, certainly not in their own businesses. I had barriers for years in corporates, I was constantly banging my head against the glass ceiling. But if you want to do something, you get out there and do it. I have to admit when I got pregnant I thought it would be revolting for doing business and attending meetings. I was totally wrong. It's all about mindset. When I was in a meeting I was there to do a job. It didn't matter that I couldn't actually reach the boardroom table, I was there.

I've got no idea how having a baby is going to change things. The reality has only just set in at eight months that I am having a baby! Up until now I've just been ignoring it. For the first five months of the pregnancy I was in the States, travelling, working, being sick as a dog and feeling like absolute death and nobody there knew. It's not something I brought up. Even here a lot of people just thought I'd put on weight. I see having children as an enhancement to your life, not for it to be a hassle. I know it's going to be different and I know it's going to be hard, I don't have rose tinted glasses on. I am committed to having a child and also committed to the company. I absolutely love what I do and I think you can be passionate about more than one thing. I won't be able to put in the same huge hours because that wouldn't be fair, but I don't see myself giving up, either. Inkspot Digital is too much a part of my life and too much a part of my personality. Everything I love is based around this business.

I fully believe if you want something get out there and create it for yourself. You can influence situations and make changes happen. Don't wait for others to do it for you – that applies if you're working for someone else or for your own company – you could be waiting a very long time and be incredibly disappointed by life. Life is for living, so live it!

Something I think is really important in whatever you choose to do with your life is personality. A lot of emphasis is placed on what you learn in school and what qualifications you have. Remember school isn't for everyone and a degree isn't everything. I was an average student. I left school after the sixth form, begrudgingly spent a year at Polytech learning to type (my mother wanted me to be a secretary!) and then two weeks after my nineteenth birthday I went overseas. Travelling really taught me a lot about myself. I learnt far more from the university of life than I could ever have learnt from an institution. This re-confirmed a belief I still have "that personality will get you a lot further in life than the ability to remember page after page of a school textbook!" I believe that with the right attitude you can learn anything, but you cannot learn to have a personality! Having a personality, being personable and being able to tailor myself to certain situations has saved me many times in business and in life generally.

Another key thing, I feel, is to have your own personal definition of what it means to be "successful". Success is relative. Maybe for you being successful means being a wonderful mother, maybe it means being a hot-shot sales person, maybe it means leading a huge corporate. Whatever success means for you, I believe you need intelligence, product and market knowledge, integrity, and the drive to see things through, even on the hard days. It took me a long time to realise that intelligence is different from being "brainy". You can be intelligent without ever having been "brainy" at school.

There are so many fantastic opportunities in this world waiting to be created and maximised. There are no barriers if you don't allow them, just challenges to be solved in a new and creative way. Give whatever it is you want your very best shot. Love what you do. And, always remember to laugh!

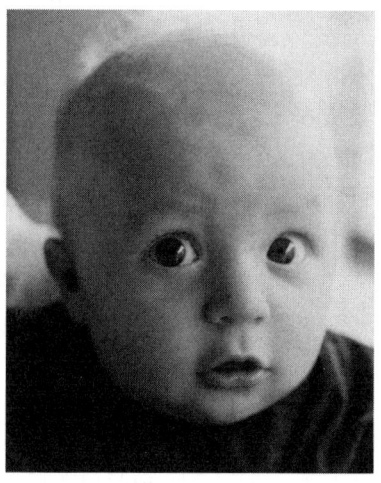

Victoria Riddiford

Victoria Riddiford

GALLERY VC

Victoria is a believer in creating your own reality. When she went into business with her close friend, Celia Kennedy, it was to create a business that would match their chosen lifestyles and was capable of fulfilling their dreams. They had a tough time with their first gallery, but revisited their vision and decided to try again in a new location. Their efforts have paid off and they're now expanding across the Tasman.

I am a firm believer that we create our own reality, so if you want to do something, get out there and do it. I think that's also a New Zealand mentality, that enthusiasm for giving something a go. It seems to be easier in New Zealand to start a business than in other places in the world. Many people I've spoken to internationally wouldn't even consider opening a business in their countries. It doesn't seem like such a big deal here, maybe it's just that 'she'll be right' Kiwi attitude.

Celia is a dear friend of mine from a long time ago. Over the years our paths have crossed quite a bit, we have been through wonderful times together and some difficult times, too. Before we went into business together, I was living in Queenstown and had two small children. Celia would come and visit me and she fell in love with the place. It's always been her dream to open her own gallery and I had a background in performing arts. Eventually we said 'why don't we just do it?' So we did.

Before we did anything else, we sat down individually and looked at our dreams, what we wanted in our lives, and what our perfect life would look like. Then we brainstormed all our personal ideas, wants, dreams and desires on a big piece of paper. It was quite visionary and quite specific. It included things like where we were living, who was around us, what we were doing. Then we looked at the potential of the business to see if it would match our dreams. We had to think about whether the gallery was going to be able to satisfy our dreams because if not, then we were heading in the wrong direction and there was no point even starting. To have a business, you have to work really hard and if it's not in line with your dreams and desires you won't have the energy for it. Some people set up businesses solely to make money. As well as financial reasons, we had other more holistic and personal reasons.

We decided that the gallery did have the potential to fulfil our dreams — that was our start point. Our initial idea was based on desire, joy and pleasure rather than economics. The reason we decided to do it here was because we wanted to live in Queenstown. We wanted to be in control of a business, and not employed by somebody else.

We wanted our business to be flexible, so we could have children in our lives as well. We based it completely on what we wanted it to be.

So we decided we would do it. Celia is great. She's the sort of person where you're either in 500% or you're not in at all. I got a bit nervous at one stage, just before we put it all on paper. I was thinking about the financial commitment and it was starting to worry me a bit. Celia phoned me and said 'I'm going to give you 24 hours to make up your mind. If you decide yes, you have to be in 100%, if you say no, then fine, but you have to make up your mind, I don't want you dithering. Just make a decision and stick with it.' Celia has a great ice cream analogy – chocolate or vanilla, it doesn't really matter which one you choose, you just have to choose one. So I said 'what the hell', jumping off the cliff, 'let's do it'. So I was in 100%. I remember that day vividly — it was scary.

My relationship with Celia is vital in this business. We are very supportive of each other. Everyone said to us 'don't go into business with your best friend, it will be disastrous.' I did consider that, but I decided to try it. I think it's actually strengthened our relationship. We are both very good communicators, we say what's up. That's vital. There are times when we drive each other completely bananas and it can be quite hard to say what's bugging us, but we have to say it, then it's sorted, and the problem is cleared. We are both very aware we don't want our business to be detrimental to our relationship. We're always there for each other no matter what happens, that's always been a primary concern.

I wouldn't try and do this by myself. It's great to have someone else to brainstorm with. I think two heads are definitely better than one. We bring different strengths to the business, and if one of us is down, the other is usually up. We both have children now, and we have a lot of fun. It's really hard to have fun on your own, and to keep generating the energy for something. I think it's much more fun doing a business with someone else, especially someone who really cares for you.

I read a wonderful book called The E-Myth, by Michael E. Gerber. I recommend it to anyone thinking about going into business. The two of us each bring different skills to the business, and through this book we assigned each other different titles. I assigned Celia the title of Executive Director. As well as directing the business, the Executive Director's role is to have an overview of the business and make sure our dreams are being met. My role is Director. As well as our dreams we also had a vision and I think that's vital. Without that vision to go back to, it's very hard to keep going when things get tough.

As the business grew we each warmed to certain areas, which is great because they're very complimentary. I do a lot of the budgeting, financial forecasts, training, personnel, communication, and we've just set up a website, so I manage that. Celia has gone totally into display - it's really important to have the gallery looking fantastic. It's her priority to make sure everything looks gorgeous. We keep talking all the time, and we both do the things in the middle, like selling, faxing, ordering, talking to people.

We walked into the gallery pretty new. A lot of learning happened once we opened the doors. Celia had already worked in a gallery so she knew some good systems and was aware of potential loopholes. I have a varied work history from performing artist to personnel manager to advertising executive. We sat down and worked out the organization and administration of the gallery, step by step. I have a very organised mind. For me, I had to go through different possibilities of what could happen in my head, and have solutions for the problems before we needed them. Other things we just dealt with as they came up.

We also talked to lots of people, enlisted their support, involved them in what we were doing and asked lots of questions. There's a huge amount of information out there, you just have to network it. If we don't know something, we just ring someone and ask. It's amazing how quickly you can get the information. I suppose it's about being humble and not pretending you know everything. Ask for help, most people are willing to offer support where they can.

I had received some inheritance money, so I put that in. Celia had absolutely nothing, apart from a car. But she had a vision, and she enrolled me in it, so then there were two of us, and we just went for it. She had nothing to borrow money against, but she had made the decision that she would get it. I can remember putting my money in and saying 'where's yours'? She said 'I'm working on it, I haven't got it yet, but I will have it'. I was like 'Okay…but hurry up!' She went to the bank and they said 'no way, you've got nothing to back it up with'. And she said 'well actually I do, because I am going to do what I say I will do'. So she went and got guarantors to support her bank loan. She split it up and got three different people to guarantee a certain amount of money. It was a matter of thinking of a clever way around the problem. She talked to a lot of people, asked them to help her and they said yes. Celia is a good woman, with a lot of integrity, and when someone has such passion and certainty about something, it's very hard to turn them down. She would put herself completely on the line for these people, no matter what happened she would pay them off.

The initial costs of the gallery were for the fitout, the stock and the stationery. Celia had an idea of what the first month's takings could be, so we had an idea of how much stock to buy. And you have to pay people. We decided to pay ourselves each week regardless. We agreed on an amount that was the bare minimum we needed to function, plus a little bit extra. We couldn't have afforded to work for less. So no matter how good or bad the business was going, we paid ourselves that drawing by automatic payment. A lot of people don't agree with that, but that's how we decided to do it. Another book I read was Rich Dad, Poor Dad by Robert T. Kiyosaki & Sharon L. Lechter, and he says to pay yourself first, and then pay everybody else with what's left.

Our first location was really tough. Initially we thought it was okay, but after three years it was killing us. It was stressful, we had people hounding us for money. Many successful retailers had closed around us, so it was obvious the location was the problem. That was our hardest time. We revisited our vision and thought about whether we wanted to give it another go. We kept brainstorming until it was obvious that we did want to try again, but we had to move. That was a big ask, energy wise, but we knew the gallery could do better.

Getting out of that location was difficult, and it got quite nasty. Our landlord had the power to be completely ruthless with us. A lot of it was about playing games really, and I'm not a game player. When things get tough like that, I think it's really important to take some action, any action, just do something to try and solve the problem. It was very clear we had to leave, so we had to find a new location, and that's what we did. We started hunting. We got out there and banged on people's doors. Even people that weren't listed with real estate agents, we'd ask them if they wanted to get out, because we wanted to get in.

I don't know how we coped during that time. It was a horrible feeling of desperation. We had to just keep talking to people, making phone calls, any action towards the result we wanted. Although it's really difficult, it's much better if you can move something, rather than just stay in a stalemate situation. We cried a lot, but we were a huge support for each other. If one of us was really down, the other would always be there to just listen, not offer advice, but really listen and acknowledge the other person's feelings.

We did consider getting out of the business. Celia had just had a baby and I'd just come back from a holiday in Switzerland, but it came down to making a decision again – chocolate or vanilla? And what else were we going to do, curl up and die? We chose chocolate and found a location within two weeks. We've never looked back since.

Celia always had a strong vision of how she wanted the gallery to look, and the feel, the intuition and the energy of the gallery. That formula has developed for me. I had a great appreciation for art and I loved colour and design, but I had never worked in a gallery, so apart from my own appreciation I didn't know anything. I share that vision completely now, we both know when something doesn't fit. The vision, knowing what something will look and feel like, is important when we're buying stock and displaying it. 'The look' is all we really have that sets us apart from anybody else. The actual administration is just like any other business.

We are very much a people business, not just a retail outlet. Our business has a lot to do with relationships, between Celia and myself, and between customers, artists and staff. Both Celia and I have trained specifically in communication, so we understand each other quite well. We both realise the importance of acknowledging people and relationships. We spend a lot of time nurturing these relationships. I think that's one of the keys to our success. It's also very satisfying, we have wonderful relationships with so many different people.

Through communication and acknowledgement we've also had wonderful relationships with our staff. In the beginning, we had one part-time staff member. We were open such long hours, and I had two small children so I didn't want to work weekends or evenings. We decided to employ someone. That was the only time we ever advertised; all our other staff have walked in and asked for a job. My background was in personnel, so I used to hire a lot of people for a big company. It was all based on the CV and whether their personality fitted. In the gallery we don't go by any of that. A person walks in and they've either got it, and fit in perfectly, or they haven't. We've been really lucky with people just walking in and getting the job. Spending the time to get clear on who or what you want is really important, though, and we are very specific.

Our staff have been brilliant. We let them know everything about the business, there're no closed books. We also give them quite a bit of responsibility, so they can feel a sense of pride and achievement in what they're doing. Because it's a small business, there is a big overlap in staff duties. We all get in there and clean the toilet or do whatever needs to be done. Our main responsibility is to have the gallery looking gorgeous and give the customer a great experience when they walk through the door.

We've had a lot of support from various people along the way. My partner has been incredibly supportive, especially in looking after our children while I've been working. He even looked after Celia's son as well, when Celia and I went away on a business trip. Juggling a business and children is hard work. I don't think I could do it without such a supportive partner. He has also been involved in the gallery fit-outs and has done a lot of work on our website. His help and input has been invaluable.

Other people have walked into the gallery, liked what we're doing and offered to help us if we need it. One thing Michael Hill (Michael Hill Jeweller) said that intuitively stuck in my brain was, 'get people who care about you involved as much as possible, like your family'. When my sister was over here, she made noises about coming back to live on this side of the world. I mentioned she could help us in Sydney. She phoned us from London to say that she wanted to do it, so that's great. I know I can completely trust her on the other side of the Tasman to be working for our cause.

Now that the gallery is busier we have moved more into director type roles, and away from frontline sales. It's quite hard to take that step back, because it means you have to employ someone else to actually create the sale. My role as Director involves a lot of paperwork and people management. Before I found it quite hard to get the paperwork done in the gallery, with people coming and going and phones ringing, but I didn't think the business could afford not to have me there generating income. The opposite has happened – I've delegated more and sales are up. I now spend my time at the gallery monitoring and inspiring the staff.

Our role is now much more management oriented. We make sure our staff are well trained and happy, and oversee quality control. Through delegating more sales responsibility to our staff, we've gained the freedom to think about new directions for the business. Without letting our production roles go, we couldn't have even considered opening in Sydney.

We opened the Sydney gallery in October 2000. From day one the bigger vision has always been to open galleries in Australia, and Sydney was the obvious first choice. We spent two years looking for the right location in Sydney. Location is absolutely vital – we've been burned and learned by a bad location in the past. We looked at so many locations but there was always something wrong with them. When my sister moved from London to Sydney we enlisted her help. She found the right one in July. She phoned me on a Friday and said 'you have got to get over here, now'. We flew to Sydney the next day and it was a really magical weekend. From the moment we walked into this place we could 'see' the gallery there, the gut feeling was right, this was the one.

The areas in Sydney are quite difficult to differentiate. Initially we were looking in Oxford Street, but there was a dichotomy there. In the busy part of Oxford Street, where the foot traffic was good, there were only very tiny (and very expensive) gallery spaces, there was no parking and security was an issue. I am a foot traffic queen, but Celia believed we could focus on getting clients to come to us. The space we chose is still in Oxford Street but in the next block over. There is less foot traffic but it's a nicer area.

In the middle of setting up the Sydney gallery we decided to change the gallery name. Up until that point we had been the Celia Kennedy Gallery. In the beginning I was quite happy with the business being named after Celia. I felt having a person's name in the business was quite personal and gave the business strength. Celia was also quite well known in the New Zealand art world, which gave us added credibility. After four years, though, I felt it was time for my name to be reflected in the business as well. As we were expanding, Celia also felt it was a good time to remove her personal name from the business. We decided to change the name, but what to? It took us a while to come up with it. We sat down and simply free associated for a while, just loosening our minds. Celia said she quite liked the symbol of the letter V, from there we came up with Gallery VC. Then it was a mad panic to get all the stationery changed in time for the Sydney gallery to open!

The hardest thing about opening the second gallery is that you're straight back to Square 1. You have to learn everything all over again, and crank things up from ground level. One of the big questions for me is "What is it that makes our gallery different? What is that makes us successful?" We need to try and define our x factor so we can replicate it in Sydney. Celia loves the challenge of starting again. She has made the choice to move to Sydney, while I focus on Queenstown.

Celia and I have strong spiritual beliefs. Not so much religious but a reverence and acknowledgement of things beyond the physical. By applying our beliefs to our business we get to test them and ourselves in a wider arena and that's so inspiring. I have learnt so much about myself, and life generally, in the process. I have learnt to trust myself, and my intuition, a lot more in all that I do. It has helped me to relax and allow the answers and support to come to me. This is incredibly liberating, freeing up time that I would otherwise spend worrying about things. While I do believe we create our own reality, I also think there is another element. When you want something you can ask the universe for help. "Speak it, act as if it's meant to be, and then allow it to fall into place."

Our business is creative, it's constantly being reinvented, and I think that's important. Every so often we open the box and brainstorm possibilities. We never limit ourselves. We brainstorm the most extraordinary possibilities we can create in our mind. I feel we create the future to step into — it has nothing to do with the past, so why limit yourself? If you can have that, you can have this, it's all the same process. There will be learning curves that crop up all of a sudden — you just have to keep going. It's all a process, a personally expanding process that Celia and I embrace wholeheartedly. It incorporates our loves, our hopes, our passions – it is our life!

Mary Murray

Mary Murray

PARADISOS CAFÉ

Mary was a fulltime mother and housewife for all 24 years of her married life until her husband announced he was having an affair. Left with nothing when he left, with no experience or business acumen whatsoever, Mary took on the café her husband had been in the process of starting, complete with thousands of dollars worth of debts, and made a go of it.

When I took on this business I had absolutely no idea about running a café, I didn't even know how to pour a filter coffee. At the time I had been married for 24 years and I was a housewife. My husband was in business and throughout my married life I'd worked the odd day here and there, but they were only pretend jobs. Earning money wasn't a side of my marriage I had to address.

My husband was setting up the café. The lease was up for renegotiation. He was going to take on the lease, do up the café, and then resell the lease. Right in the middle of it all he announced he was having an affair, that he was going to be leaving, and he wanted the business sold. He really didn't want me in the café, but I dug my toes in. Bearing in mind that I suddenly had no source of income, no house, and I had been a housewife for the last 24 years, I decided I had to give it a go.

It was tough. While they finalised the details, I had to work with my husband and his new girlfriend. Emotionally, I wasn't the best equipped to deal with anything, let alone running a business.

My first real insight into how little business acumen I had, and how little support I was about to have, was when I had to go to the bank. I had to take over the overdraft with my father as guarantor. When I went to the bank they talked to my father, not to me. I don't think Dad really wanted to lend me the money, I suspect he was looking for an out. The bank certainly didn't want to lend money to a middle-aged housewife, on the verge of a breakdown, who didn't have an ounce of business acumen. That was my first introduction to how difficult it was going to be for me as a woman, without a house or any collateral. My husband had taken everything.

Eventually my father agreed to act as a guarantor, even though the bank advised him I was a dodgy prospect. I think he felt sorry for me at the time so he gave it a go, which I am grateful for. I repaid his trust, and his money, and from there I constantly grew. When I came into the business, I found I was left with thousands of dollars of debts I had been completely unaware of. So as well as struggling to come to terms with every other aspect of the business — staff, wages, GST — I constantly had creditors ringing me demanding money. At any one time, they could have put me under so I had no choice but to get a grasp on everything as quickly as possible.

I was extremely fortunate to have the support of my daughter, Emily. She was at university, studying for a masters degree at the time. She quickly came to terms with many aspects of running the business. My husband had left nothing. Emily set the books up, started doing costings, and thought it was feasible, that if we got it right we could make a go of it. Emily worked out what it would cost me to run the business and said, "Mum this is what you have to do every week before you even turn the lights on, otherwise you're going to be in trouble."

I initially worked seven days a week, from 5.20 in the morning, until 7 at night. Gradually I made myself completely au fait with every aspect of running this café. Every day was a battle, until now it's easier. Now I don't owe anyone anything, I run my business on a monthly accounts system, I have a good name around town, I make one of the best coffees in Christchurch, and most of the time I enjoy it.

I learnt through making plenty of mistakes. After 24 years of marriage I was dropped in it – I could make a go of it, or go under, that was it. I just had to carry on each day, read up on things, and educate myself. Everyday I tried to make sure the lack of knowledge I had didn't go with me into tomorrow. I set myself targets every day. The cappuccino machine used to scare the shits out of me.

Some days I'd have a queue half way down the mall, and I wouldn't know how I was ever going to get on top of it, but I did.

In the beginning all the suppliers were a bit dubious about me. They didn't want someone else coming along who wasn't going to pay their bills. They were pleasant with me because I was honest with them. I didn't have problems with them because I was female, the problems were because I owed them money. They didn't want to hear that I was a crack in the middle of the business, they wanted me to be positive. I had to accept that I would have to start dealing on a cash only basis until they believed in me. So I went through that process. Once they saw I was meeting their demands, it was okay. I don't have any trouble now, but I wouldn't take it now, either. Back then I was just so meek and grateful that they would let me stay in business another week. It's not to their benefit to put anyone under, they'd be left getting five cents in the dollar, instead of their full dollar!

I think the only reason I survived when I first came into business was that I was honest. Once I became familiar with the creditors that were hounding me, I made myself ring every creditor once a week and ask them for leniency. I'd say, " please bear with me another week, I'll make sure you get $27 this week, I won't take any drawings myself, but I'll get us out of here, I believe I can do it." It was hard to do but they'd say that phone call was worth two payments.

I came to terms with the ramifications of the business I took on being very shakey. Now it's become stronger, I think maybe it was a healthier way to start. With a business that's buoyant and all cashed up, it's probably easier to become flippant.

The only support I had was Emily, who had a lot more savvy than I did at the time. She believed in me and every day she'd say, "never look at how far you've got to go, look at how far you've already come. You can make it grow, we can make it successful." I'm sure there's a lot of support and information out there for small businesses, but I simply didn't have the time. I was working fourteen hours a day, seven days a week, so I wasn't in a position to tap into anything.

I now employ 21 staff and do my best to make the café a happy working environment. Behind every business there's an engineroom of wonderful women. Take my dishwasher. It's bloody hard work, it's highly underpaid and under acknowledged, but without her I couldn't run my business. Without the sandwich makers, without the person who clears the tables, these women are all vital and are the unsung heroes of New Zealand businesses. I have women who work here and do a great job without a lot of recognition. And they go on to do several other jobs, as well as having a husband to attend to, kids to look after, housework to do. I believe that is what makes all businesses in New Zealand successful – the tuggers out there in the engineroom.

In choosing my staff I like to spend some time with them. I don't believe in references. I usually know when I meet them, it's very much a one-on-one gauge. A lot of people come to me by word of mouth. I ask my staff if they know anyone like them, maybe other ladies at home who'd like a few hours work.

I employ two men and they're both superb. I was slightly hesitant to employ them because it's largely a female domain here, but they've been great. I have been enormously fortunate with my staff, with the exception of one. Most have stayed on, so I have a very low turnover. I want them to be my friends. I have to trust them, as they feel they can trust me. I try to be as malleable as I possibly can. A lot of my staff are women with children and I always try and fit in with their needs, because I want them to work here and I want them to be happy. I don't want staff here just thinking about how much money they have to earn for the week. I want them to be able to go home after work and think that was quite a good day.

I don't think I'm a hard taskmaster. There isn't really a boss, we're all here doing a job. I have to take responsibility for them, but that's really the only way I see myself as the boss. I have to work harder than anyone else because at the end of the day it's not the staff's problem, it's my problem. If they are poor at their job, that's a reflection on me. I have to clearly state my needs when I take someone on and my needs have to be met.

As far as menus and pricing go, I adjusted everything when I started. The food is completely different. It's all based on common sense really. The customers tell you very quickly what they like and don't like. If you've got a cabinet full of food at the end of the day, it's for one reason – they didn't like it, you didn't make it properly. I might have tolerated that for a fortnight before thinking I've got to improve this. So I asked the customers, what was wrong, what didn't they like. Now if something doesn't sell twice, I address it. I can't afford to have it, I can't afford for them not to want it. You just have to use your common sense and intuition to get a feel for it.

Before getting into this business I'd never had any experience in dealing with solicitors, accountants, or the Inland Revenue Department. Most I found to be helpful and obliging. I think they were pleasant because I was honest and I owed them money. The IRD were excellent. They allowed me to pay debts off. Their sole purpose wasn't to destroy me. They took on board my lack of business knowledge and skills, and my lack of articulation with them. They explained things to me, and allowed me to pay so much a week until I honoured that debt, and then they moved on.

I owed the solicitor and accountant money, unbeknown to me. I owed rent to the mall, which I knew nothing about. And, just when I thought I was out of the quagmire, someone else would come along with another bill. Everyone was impressed when I paid the debts and they're impressed today when I go in with the books and show a healthy business that's growing. I don't have to be scared of anyone, or anything, now. In the first year, I'd be terrified every time the phone would ring, thinking 'oh no, who will it be today. Who have I not acknowledged because I don't know I owe them money'. And I was too scared to get things fixed when they broke down because then I'd owe someone else money.

Even once I had the business on track I still had trouble with the banks. The bank I had been dealing with in the mall closed, as so many small branches did. After a time of driving to the next closest bank four days a week for change, I knew I wasn't going to hack it. So I approached another bank in the mall. It was two years down the track and I had books to prove I had more business acumen than I had originally, but I still went through the same shit. I didn't have any collateral still because I didn't have a house. But, they'd seen my banking records, they'd seen my growth, they'd seen my capabilities at paying debts structurally and keeping a business afloat. It still didn't have any affect because I was a forty six year old woman in business who had no house, and no male backing. They didn't want to know about it so now, after a struggle, I run a business without an overdraft.

Every day there are hurdles, some bigger than others. Last year I was closed for three months while they did renovations to the mall. They shut me down with one weeks notice! The site was completely obliterated as the whole mall was revamped – I was just a casualty of it. There was no legal redress, the lease was made out entirely in their favour. It was like anything in life – if you don't like it leave, if you want to make something out of it, stay and make something out of it. My staff were paid for the three months so I had them to come back to. In fact after three months it was me that didn't want to come back, I didn't think I could face it. But after a couple of days, you forget the three months you've had off and you're back in gear again.

I used that time to make myself more familiar with what other cafés were selling, a lot more competitive, and a lot more structured. I also recharged my energy. It was a nightmare at the time, but it's forgotten now, along with all the other bad things that happen. You can do without these things, but they happen, and you just have to carry on and cope as best you can. Once upon a time I would have gone out the back and cried every time something bad happened, now I just get on with it.

The key to success is giving the food and service that people want. The hospitality industry in Christchurch is so over-geared to cater for everyone. There're more cafes in Christchurch than there are in Melbourne, with a much smaller population base. It's a very cut throat business. You just have to be so much better than the next person because you're all offering the same thing. All I can offer that is better is service and staff training, making sure the food looks good and the presentation is superb. That's really the only reason I'm still here today. It certainly isn't because I've got some sugar daddy behind me.

I'm not the same person who came here four years ago. I'm far more confident and articulate. I know that I am good at what I do and that it's successful. I have achieved something I never could've achieved before. I don't have a particular mentor, I admire any woman who's a hard worker. I do this for myself. I never want to go back to that little me that was too frightened and felt too insignificant to make a filter coffee. I have proven to myself, and to my children who had faith in me, that yes, I am capable of running a business. From where I came from within myself, I am completely unrecognisable. I would never go back to any of that, or to relying on being given $100 a week and not knowing where the rest of the money went.

I've gained personal confidence, financial independence, new friends. I never have to answer to anyone else, my mistakes are my own, and when I go home I don't have to worry about other things going on in other people's lives. Through this business, I have grown in every possible healthy way. I can look people in the eye. I can meet with the bank manager or the solicitor. I'm not scared anymore. Knowledge is such power. When I first started I was a jibbering idiot, constantly running out the back crying because I couldn't cope. I can deal with things now. This wouldn't have been possible without the enormous support of my daughter, because she believed in me, and stood with me.

It was two years in business before I felt confident that I wouldn't get taken out by any of my creditors. And my landlords — after two years I wasn't scared of them either. For the first year they knew I was scared of them so of course they had a field day. But then I thought right, I'll show them I've got as much balls as they have. I'll state my needs and play within the parameters they set, but I'm not scared of them. Once I set those standards to myself, I found I wasn't scared of them, I could sit there and say no, I'm not doing that, I don't agree with this, and sure, I'm happy to do that.

Also I was disciplined. I couldn't afford to pull back until I was sure I had everything tidied. Then I could give myself time off and a wage adequate to my lifestyle. I was constantly doing checks and balances along the way. I never ran before I could walk. I was never scared to ask for advice, or to say when I didn't know what to do next. It doesn't matter what type of business you're in, if you're a good hard worker and you use common sense, there's no reason why you shouldn't succeed. It's when you want to go too big, too fast, you're dishonest about what you take out of the business, you don't put money back into the business, or you're not attending to your customers needs, that is when you fail. And that is the same for all businesses.

If the opportunity comes, seize it. If I can do it, anybody can. Don't be frightened. Don't stay in a bad marriage, move on if that's what you have to do. We can all leave, we can all change our situation. Move on, and if you're not going to move on, then make the most of what you've got.

I would say to anyone considering going into business, DO IT! Believe in yourself. Enjoy it for the opportunity it has given you. It doesn't matter if you don't make lots of money out of it, it matters that you're contributing something worthwhile as a person, and your life is more interesting because of it. Embrace it. Enjoy it. Go for it. Take out of it what you need. We are all worthwhile. There is not a woman out there who couldn't do it, there truly isn't. You just have to want to do it.

Jacqui Thomas

Jacqui Thomas

WRITER / PUBLISHER / EVENT ORGANISER

After two university degrees and years spent wandering around the world, Jacqui finally worked out what she wanted to do with her life – go into business for herself. This book has been a huge learning curve - in writing, in publishing and in business generally. Part way through this project she took an opportunity to help organise an international event and thinks she may have finally discovered her niche in event management. Who knows what the future may bring!

It was only recently that the option of working for myself finally dawned on me. All through school it was expected that I would go to university and come out the other end being something. The only trouble was I didn't know what it was I wanted to 'be'. I started studying law and hated it, the next year I decided to do psychology. For a while I thought I'd probably become a clinical psychologist, that was until I spent a year doing volunteer counselling and decided I didn't have the patience to deal with other people's problems all day, every day! I spent four years at Canterbury University and finished with two degrees but still no idea what I was going to do with them. By the end I was really just working towards getting the damn piece of paper so I could escape and go travelling overseas.

I spent the next four years travelling and doing all sorts of different jobs from working on a yacht in the Whitsundays, to teaching English in Korea, to accounting in London, selling jewellery in Asia, working on ski-fields, and the good old backstop - waitressing. I thought that in a big city like London, the job of my dreams might appear, but it didn't and eventually I came home to New Zealand and decided to live in Queenstown.

I'd lived in Queenstown a couple of times before and loved the energy of the place. The only trouble with living in Queenstown is that employment options are really limited to tourism and hospitality. I did my time waitressing and selling jetboat rides but wanted something more. By this stage it was ten years since I'd left school and I still had no idea where I was heading. I knew I was intelligent and had so much to offer the world. I knew I was worth more than ten bucks an hour but had no idea how to convince other people of that!

Finally, my eyes were opened to the option of working for myself. I met Noel Coutts, entertainer and local icon. He worked for a few hours most nights doing something he loved, he had the days to himself to do whatever he pleased and he earned in a night what I was slogging away for a week to make. This was the answer, being self employed - but what was I going to do? Journalism was an option I'd toyed with for a while at school – I think somewhere in between wanting to be a pharmacist and a lawyer. I'd enjoyed English at school and it seemed like something I could do from Queenstown. I enrolled in a correspondence course and I was away, I loved it. I was amazed when my first stories were published. In the beginning I was so nervous when I had to ring people for comments or to arrange interviews. I would say I'm Jacqui Thomas, a freelance journalist writing a story for such and such, and I was sure they'd think I wasn't a real journalist. I felt like a fake. Noel helped me through my phone call fears through a little trick of imagining people in the toilet. I don't use it very often these days, but I have to say it works! No-one seems very scary when you imagine them sitting on the toilet! It's a very good reminder that no matter how important someone might seem, they're only human just like you and me. I also quickly realised that people have no reason to doubt you unless you give them one. If you can write a real story you can be a real journalist and that goes for anything.

One of my biggest mistakes in the beginning was being afraid to ask people for help. I wanted people to take me seriously so I felt I had to pretend I knew what I was doing. I knew I could write the story, that wasn't the problem, but the business side of it was – I didn't have a clue! Through researching this book I've learned that it's so important to ask questions, and people are generally happy to help you with the answers. There is absolutely no need to be wandering blindly along by yourself. Ask questions - nine times out of ten, people will be only too happy to help. And, if you don't get the answer, ask someone else, you'll get the information you need eventually.

I think my perception of successful people has always been that they just knew what to do. I don't know whether I thought they were born with this knowledge or whether I just thought they were successful because of the type of people they are. The truth is nobody is born knowing how to be successful, we all start off the same. These people are successful because they have asked questions, they have learned along the way. Nobody knew how to succeed before they started. Through interviewing all these successful women I was constantly surprised to find they started off just like me – at the bottom, not knowing all the answers, and they've learned and through this they've become successful.

I must credit my dear friend Noel for encouraging me along the way and in fact being the impetus for this book. It was him who suggested writing this book, he invested in the project, he has been there to give me a push whenever I've needed it and he inspired the title by constantly encouraging me to "Go, Girl, Go!" It is so important to have the support of people around you. Enrol them in your projects - get the people you care about behind you, their support is invaluable.

Through this project I've learned so much, not just how to write a book but all sorts of things about myself and other people. In researching this book I met some amazing women. In fact there wasn't a single woman I didn't come away from without having learned something.

One of the things I've learned along the way is a little embarrassing. I've discovered that I don't want to be a fulltime writer anymore. Initially I thought "Oh, no, I made such a big deal about telling people that I am a writer and people finally accept that that's what I am, what I do. Now I have to turn around and announce to the world that I'm not a writer, I'm something else." I'm over that, now. Through writing and especially through working on this book, I've discovered other things that I'm good at and that I enjoy. Writing is a skill I will always have and I will continue to use it, but as part of a bigger picture rather than as my sole focus. I think it's important to be flexible in business - some of the best ideas have evolved over time. Who knows what may be waiting around the corner – what you thought was your ultimate goal may just be a stepping stone to something bigger and brighter you haven't even thought of yet.

Last year I took a wonderful opportunity to help organise an international event in Queenstown. From the minute I heard about the position I knew it was for me. This was like the dream job I had been hoping would one day appear, not the sort of job you see advertised in a newspaper. I had to wait though, for the friend who had mentioned it to me to decide that she wasn't interested. I knew she wasn't in the headspace to take it, she'd just finished a huge job that had been really draining. I knew it was meant for me, but I had to wait for her to decide. By the time she had decided, the position had been advertised – so how was I going to convince them that I was the right person? I sent some gourmet jellybeans with my application and hoped I could convince them of my passion and enthusiasm for the position. I'm not sure whether they could feel my energy or whether the jellybeans worked but they gave me the contract and I started working on the inaugural Compaq 50K of Coronet.

This was my foray into event management. With the support of top level sponsors, we brought eight international teams of world-class downhill ski racers to New Zealand for a 16 hour endurance ski event. We incorporated other supporting events to make a week of it. The aim of the entire event was to raise money for a new brand charity we created called "Cure Kids". We also brought six "Cure Kids" representatives and their parents to Queenstown for the trip of a lifetime. For the next three months, this event was my life, and I loved it. As well as the sponsors, local businesses and hundreds of volunteers, I worked with three amazing people –

Wayne Cafe, Fraser Skinner and Jeff Turner, all successful in their own business areas, and all incredibly passionate about making the event a success. I owe it to these guys for giving me a wonderful opportunity and helping me learn so much in such a short time.

This brings me to another point - make the most of all of your resources, especially human ones. Ask people you respect and admire for help and advice. By giving people an opportunity to help you, as well as learning from them, you also make them feel good. It's very rewarding to be able to help someone or offer advice – usually they'll feel honoured that you respect their opinion. Also remember that these people didn't get to where they are on their own – other people helped them. Now, it's their turn to help others further down the line.

I really enjoyed working on the Compaq 50K and I know I did a good job because I can honestly say I put my whole self into it. I believe when you truly put your heart and soul into something and give 120% of your self then you can only but succeed. From this event came other contracts and more learning curves. Starting all over again in a new business meant just that, starting again. The same questions – what to charge, how to estimate time involved on a project, what is expected of me? This time, though, I wasn't scared to ask questions, I didn't feel like I had to pretend I knew all the answers. My biggest dilemma of the moment is what to call myself. I've been putting off getting new business cards printed for months while I try and come up with a business name that feels right. Maybe this is a sign. Maybe event management is another stepping stone. The more I learn about business, the more I want to sink my teeth into something bigger and braver.

After the Compaq 50K, it was also time to pull my writing out from its box and finish this book. I have to admit it was a scary prospect

- I hadn't looked at it for months. What if I re-read the stories and thought they were awful? Thankfully, I found I still liked the concept and the stories and was re-inspired to keep going and complete the project.

It was time to continue approaching publishers. I found a publisher that was interested but was horrified to hear it would take another year before the book would reach the shelves! That, combined with the harsh reality of author royalties (a mere pittance) and the thought of handing over my pet project to someone else to take over led me to explore the option of self publishing. I realised I had already been working with an ideal publishing partner and braved myself to make the proposition. I'm sure he was wondering what on earth I could have up my sleeve when I told Jeff I had a business proposition for him. I knew he loved books and having had him proof read over my shoulder for the past few months, I knew he was a stickler for spelling and grammar. And with the Compaq 50K over, for a few months at least, I thought he'd have the time to be involved in another business venture.

Approaching him was actually quite scary. It was one thing sending your stories off to a complete stranger to reject, but giving them to a friend was a bit like walking down the main street of your hometown naked! When I told him about my idea of setting up a publishing company, with the first project being my book, he said yes straight away. It was too easy - I didn't really believe he was serious. And with that he went overseas. It wasn't until he came back and asked what was happening with our publishing company that I realised he was serious – JT Publishing Co was in business.

I think a lot of people are put off going into business because of money, lack of it. I don't have any, although I fully intend to make some. I don't think lack of funds is a valid excuse for not putting a good idea into action. There is always money out there for good ideas. Once again you have to make the most of your resources and contacts. If you have a good idea and are passionate about it, the chances are you can convince someone to invest in you. And why wouldn't they? You're offering them a share in something fantastic!

So many people have helped me along the way, too many to mention them all by name. I must credit my family, though, and in particular my Mum and Dad for giving me such a fabulous start in life. I am lucky enough to be one of the few people in my generation to still have two loving parents living in the same house. They have always supported me in whatever I've chosen to do, which I'm sure has been difficult for them sometimes, and I really do appreciate that. They gave me the start from which I've become who I am today and I hope they are proud of me. I think they are because they've finally stopped asking when I'm going to use my university degrees!

I never thought I would cope very well with having a business partner. Initially the sole reason for being self-employed was exactly that, to work for myself and not to have to answer to anyone else! Jeff has been great to work with, though and because neither of us had any experience in publishing when we started it's been fun learning together. It's nice to have someone to share the difficulties with and the triumphs. Two heads are better than one and usually you find two people have different strengths to bring to a business. While I wouldn't go into a partnership with just anybody, I definitely am enjoying it a lot more than I ever anticipated.

Other people have come to the fore lately to help get this book to the shelves. Perhaps they, like me, are ready for this project to be complete! Cay Cassini has done a wonderful job of the photographs, traipsing around the country making these women look absolutely fabulous.

Minhal, the absolute sweetheart, came to my rescue when I was having a cover crisis. The design team were despairing of me because although I knew how I wanted the cover to feel, I had no idea how I wanted it to look. Knowing what you don't want is only helpful up to a point! After wandering around a bookstore for fifteen minutes we decided that book covers in general were in crisis, and went to Minhal's studio to create something completely different and inspirational. Forty minutes later, we had the artwork for the cover – thank you Minhal! Ally and Lindsay at Niche Design have also been fantastic, so fantastic in fact that they extended my deadline until tomorrow to have this last chapter finished.

This has definitely been the hardest story to write and I acknowledge again how generous the other women in this book have been to bare their souls for us all to share and learn from. Thank you.